ICE HOCKEY IN THE DESERT
...What Was I Thinking?

The Legacy of Leo Golembiewski and the Icecats

D0111882

Leo Golembiewski and Alan M. Petrillo

Introduction by Don Rickles
Forward by Bobby Hull

Published by Leo Golembiewski and Alan M. Petrillo
P.O. Box 18402, Tucson, AZ 85731

ISBN   978-1-880677-22-3

First printing — November 2011

Cover photo by Jeff Albiniak

Dedication

Dedicated to my wife Paula for her faith and belief in me- and the pursuit of my dream.

Thanks to my Mom, Dad and brother Chet.

Introduction

Hi Hockey Pucks!

Growing up in New York, I was a big Rangers fan so when it comes to hockey, I'm no dummy. Coach G's coming to Tucson to start a hockey team what the hell was he thinking?

Only an ex-goalie from Chicago would try to start a hockey team in the desert. He must have been hit in the head too many times. Oh yeah, come to think of it, he's Polish! I thought the only ice in Arizona was in a glass. Boy, was I wrong.

After more than 30 years, the Arizona Icecats maintained a great hockey team, thanks mostly to Coach G. I was the team's honorary captain a few years back and it was an honor to be part of such a great organization.

Coach G, you're a special guy and a special friend. Thanks for being part of the documentary on my life, *Mr. Warmth — the Don Rickles Project*.

All the best,

Don Rickles

P.S. Good luck — keep pushing the puck up the ice — he shoots, he scores! I need to get a life!

Foreword

I have known Leo for more than 30 years, both as a friend and coach of the University of Arizona Icecats. The program he has built in Tucson has been a huge success in such an unexpected place. I have seen his work up close, attending not only an Icecat banquet, but serving as an Icecat Honorary Captain. Being active with the Chicago Blackhawk Alumni Association, I worked with Coach G to stage a couple of charity hockey games in Tucson.

His efforts on behalf of the sport and the creation of the Icecat hockey program is truly laudable. He has made it possible for many young, talented hockey players to receive solid educations while seeing parts of the United States they might never have seen.

He always set high standards for these young men on the ice and in the classroom, and has done it out of his love of hockey and his desire to pay forward some of the many benefits that our great game has given him.

I am happy to call Coach G a friend — a rink rat growing up in the hallways and balconies of the old Chicago Stadium. He has built such a tremendous life in hockey and has given much back to it. He's a great contributor to our sport at its very important grass roots.

Bobby Hull
"The Golden Jet"
NHL Hall of Fame, 1983

1.
Appearances

People are automatically going to think I'm a millionaire because I coach at the University of Arizona. But I can tell you that I haven't made a lot of money throughout the nearly 40 years I've been doing this. I'm so much different than other coaches at the University and around the country. I can tell you one thing for sure — I'm a man of substance. People should know about Leo G. They should know about the man and his philosophy. They should know the man behind the mask, whether it be the goalie's mask or the mask that I wear every day out in public.

When it comes to sports, whether hockey, baseball or some other sport, if you're better than the people on the other team, you beat them. The key to it is not being better than people and still beating them.

When I look at what we've done here with the Icecats, I realize we've never had a lot of depth on most of our teams. The Icecats always have been lucky simply to have two decent lines to put on the ice. I don't think we've ever had a third or fourth scoring line. Besides that, in all our years, we've never had more than four good defensemen on a team at the same time.

I don't scout other teams. Not only is it cost prohibitive, but the Icecats also don't exchange tapes with other teams. The reason for that is simple. I coach with the intent on making my guys ready and making the other team adapt to us, not making us adapt to the other team. You'll find that I don't match lines like some other coaches do. With all the Icecat personnel, we try to teach them that they have to play in a particular way, whether it's the first, second or third line. We want to get our opponents to react to us, and not us react to them.

Our forte — that of the players — is speed. If we don't bring speed to the game, then we've lost a major part of what we are and what we can accomplish. Of course, pure physical attributes are important. But you still have to go after the other team. All these years smaller players were given an opportunity to play regardless — get the job done.

There are a few things that stick in my mind — that I've learned over the years — but that still are instructive today.

For instance, Scotty Bowman, the Hall of Fame coach for the St. Louis Blues, Buffalo Sabres, Montreal Canadiens and Detroit Red Wings, told me in 1969 that motivation is the key to success. That's as true today as it was forty years ago.

Another maxim that stays in my mind is that mental preparedness will directly affect execution or the lack thereof. Physicality is a big part of hockey, but being prepared mentally is a bigger part.

For many athletes today, and particularly for most hockey players, with the way the sport is coached and taught or not taught, the mental part is something that's not addressed very frequently. But it should be.

If you're a good or even a great hockey player, you'll come up through the ranks — from pee wee through bantam, midget and then juniors because you're a good hockey player. If you get the job done, you move up the food chain based on your physical ability and execution. But when that hockey player gets to a higher level or tries to get to the ultimate level —the pros — then he's going to be scouted and the scouts will know every move the kid makes.

That's why in baseball you have scouts and checkers and you have the same thing in hockey. We try to get our players to understand that because it absolutely, positively is important to their careers.

This lack of mental preparedness cuts across all levels of all sports because the mental aspect of life in sports is not addressed. Most kids live their lives by flying by the seat of their pants. Oh, they think, it's a brand new day. Let's go. Put on the music, turn on the iPod. How are you doing, dude?

With a lot of today's kids, there's no accountability, which is part of the coaching intangibles that I have to deal with. I've found that there's no consistent accountability in most of these kids' lives. They talk to mom and dad once a week. They have tests at the University according to their syllabi. The only structure in their lives is the classes they take.

For many of these kids, getting by is keeping mom and dad off their back, and keeping their peers happy with them. Their direction is lateral. Their lives aren't upward mobility. It's getting by, being one of the boys and eventually that catches up with you.

Hockey is a vehicle that we use to try to get these kids to acknowledge discipline, to sacrifice and to adhere to all those other intangibles — being responsible, accountable and loyal. Loyal not only to yourself, not only to your family and friends, but also to all the other people in your life. Loyalty is huge!

It's tough being a student and being that age, because of the peer pressure alone. Granted, I was lucky when I was younger. I was supposed to be the family priest since I was 10 years old. I had this built-in goal that my family had formed for me. Ultimately, through my desire to be an educator and through being a Benedictine, I thought the best way for me to serve youth and kids in sports was not having to wear a priest's collar.

That goal of being a family priest — was it set by others? When you first entertain those thoughts, you have to wonder.

I had a great childhood. My brother, Chester and I, we were raised well. Our dad and mom, Chester Sr. and Irene, raised their kids with discipline, morals, values and ethics. So I was a hockey player who never drank or smoked or ever did drugs, ever. And for that matter, my brother is the same way. We never had a thought to stray to the dark side because it was simply the way we were brought up by our parents.

I remember my dad asking, "You want a beer? It's in the fridge." I remember it clearly. I tried the beer, but it tasted lousy. I never acquired a taste for it. So instead, I've been addicted to Diet Pepsi, without a doubt. When I get off the ice after practicing with one of the guys, I grab a one liter Diet Pepsi and it's an aphrodisiac for me. It doesn't get better than that.

I've been called an enigma by a number of people. I've also been called a "Renaissance Man" because I'm involved in hockey and baseball and other kinds of athletics and I'm a pack rat. I love political intrigue and especially presidential history. I have interests in everything from autographed presidential signatures to autographed baseballs, to autographed hockey pucks and baseballs from NHL Hall of Famers and Major League Baseball Hall of Famers. I have an especially soft spot for anything relating to the Chicago White Sox. I have a room in my house that you can't even walk into because I've got stuff all over the place.

I think that I'm an enigma because people don't really know who I am. I can tell you that having them not know who I am is an exceptionally great defense mechanism. If I let you into my circle and you betray that trust, then I'm the one who gets hurt, generally not you. That has happened periodically throughout my life, much to my dismay.

Think about how coaching works. I ran hockey schools and taught kids from five years old to high school. Let's say you're a 13 or 14 year old and I'm coaching you in Babe Ruth or Pony league. These kids say that Coach G, he's cool, man. He talks about no drinking, no smoking and all sorts of other things.

Then the kids get to be 16 and 17 years old, and they get a car. All of a sudden, Coach G isn't so cool any more because his stance on drinking, partying and drugs didn't change because you've turned 17. Even though their urges do.

This is tantamount to what and who I am. I've always believed, even as a high school coach of 18 year old kids, that the sooner a boy — soon to become a man — knows who he is and what he wants, the better.

And I try to help him find it.

I like to tell folks that "you can't bullshit a bullshitter." If I can sell hockey in the desert than I can sell just about anything. There are people who despise me and hate my guts because I help their kids. When the day is over, I don't really care, because I want to make a difference in these kids' lives. I try to live every day as a whole day.

When I think back about how difficult it's been in Tucson, putting this team together, holding it together and making it successful, it's tough. There is nobody in town who has eaten more crap sandwiches than Leo G, but the whole thing is not about me. I'll keep on doing what I know how to do. Do I hurt while I'm doing it? I hurt more than you can ever imagine, but it's not about me.

I like to think that I'm a black cowboy hat guy. I'm a cross between Matt Dillon of Gunsmoke and Wyatt Earp of Tombstone, and maybe even a little bit of Doc Holliday. My signature is jeans and tee shirts. When I'm behind the bench during a game, it's a black blazer, shirt and tie.

What I try to share with the kids who are playing for the Icecats is that I try to develop them. They might not like their mom and dad, for whatever reason, but that's not right. If I tell them to go jump off milepost 12 of Mt. Lemmon Hwy., they probably would because I'm their coach. Their mom and dad might tell them to drive more slowly, but they probably won't pay attention to mom and dad, or me either, but I try to be an extension of their mom and dad.

These kids today are a much tougher crowd than those who I coached 10 to 15 years ago, but the philosophy hasn't changed in my coaching. If you buy into the fact that what I believe is right for you as a man, then you'll get somewhere.

But what percentage of the Icecats buy into that?

In their hearts these players know that I'm right. The big question is how much they can wrestle with their own demons and their own peer pressure to develop wisdom? It's very difficult to answer that question.

When I played varsity baseball during my freshman year in college, and varsity tennis during my junior and senior years, I loved to practice. It wasn't unusual to find us practicing until between 10:30 and 12:30 at night.

I played baseball during my freshman year, and the next year a new coach came in and told me he didn't want me to play hockey. I said two words and they're not 'let's dance.' I wasn't swearing at that time. I didn't start swearing until after my best friend Bob Mackey got killed in an automobile accident.

If you change as a person, there is usually a pivot point for the change — a particular reason. Bob Mackey was killed on July 31 at 9:32 pm on Route 53 and Itasca Road in Itasca, Illinois. That's when I put my faith in my religion. Before that I didn't use the word, shit. Never. Read my lips — never.

What's really important? The way you talk or the way you orchestrate your life and your actions really is most important.

After Bob died I put my faith in religion in order to make my life work. Bob was 18 and so was I. Bob's girlfriend was 17. I tried to help her go on with her life. That is what really changed me in the context of drawing me into the idea that I could probably better help people in the outside world than in the monastic community.

One thing I can tell you is that I'm very stick-to-it. When I was in seventh grade I think I won the Stick-to-it Award. I say that because I never give up. I always liked the Bobby Kennedy poster from my college days — "It's Not Why . . . It's Why Not!" I don't like being told, "no." I want to find a way to make that word a "yes."

The one thing I can absolutely tell you is that it's been an interesting run.

2.
A Hockey Idol

The man who Coach G considers his most influential friend is a man who's name is inextricably linked with hockey lore — Glenn Hall, a 1975 inductee into the NHL Hall of Fame and longtime goalie for the Detroit Red Wings, Chicago Black Hawks and St. Louis Blues.

Hall is especially notable for developing the goaltending style referred to as the "butterfly" technique where the goaltender protects the lower part of the net by dropping to his knees and spreading his pads, simultaneously flaring his glove and stick arms and hands to protect the upper net. Such a technique evoked the outline of a butterfly and thus the name of the technique was born.

A young Leo Golembiewski was especially moved by the style, flair, technique and performance of Hall, so much so that Leo strove as a young man to be everything that he felt Hall embodied. When on the ice, Leo attempted to emulate Hall. When off the ice, Leo still wanted to be like the man who he would look up to as a hockey god.

"I first met Leo when I was playing for the Chicago Black Hawks," Hall says. "I met him after a game. He came up to me and was eager to ask a lot of questions. He was a young kid, full of enthusiasm and eager to improve himself and his game."

Hall says he remembers Leo as an avid hockey fan.

"You could tell that he was a pretty intelligent young man, with ideas of what he wanted to do with his career and his life," Hall says. ""But I don't think anyone would ever have thought that he would go to the desert and start a successful hockey team there."

Hall notes that he visited Coach G in Tucson a couple of times with his now-deceased wife, Pauline, to celebrate various Arizona Icecats milestones at banquets.

"Even though I was a Cubs fan when I was in Chicago, when I was in Tucson for spring training, when the White Sox came up to bat, I rooted for them anyway, just like Leo did," Hall pointed out.

Hall believes that Leo patterned himself much after St. Louis Blues coach Scotty Bowman.

"In my opinion, Scotty was the smartest hockey coach who ever coached," Hall says. "He treated his players well too, even though he was a tough coach. There was never a guy who wasn't a better player after playing for Scotty."

That style of coaching had its effect on Leo, Hall believes.

"Leo is a really solid guy who expects discipline and total effort from his players," Hall says. "He's very intense like Scotty, lives and breathes hockey 24 hours a day, 7 days a week. He's totally dedicated."

Hall continues, "I see many of Scotty Bowman's qualities in Leo. I can see clearly how he patterned himself after Scotty and how well he has lived those qualities."

3.
Family Insights

Coach G's mom, Irene Golembiewski, has lived in Tucson since 1973 when she and her late husband, Chester Sr., (who died in 1976), moved to Tucson. As might be expected, Irene has fond memories of her eldest son as a child.

"He's always been a good kid," she says. "He's very dependable, used to do his schoolwork well, and loved to play baseball. I never had any problems with Leo."

Both Leo and younger brother Chet had paper routes when they were in public grammar school, Irene points out, which she believes helped them develop confidence in their abilities to make their own way in the world.

"Leo was a serious type of individual," Irene notes. "No matter what he did, he applied himself — sports like baseball and hockey, and of course his schoolwork. He always made sure his schoolwork was done so he could play baseball or hockey."

Irene laughs when asked about Leo's dream of creating a hockey team for American-born players in the Southwestern desert.

"People never thought that there could be hockey in Tucson that would last any amount of time," Irene says, "but Leo got it going and has continued it in good fashion. Once he starts something, he keeps going. He doesn't quit — he never puts things aside, he just gets them done."

Leo's cousin in Wisconsin, Myron Golembiewski, remembers Leo staying summers on their farm.

"He came for several years, around the age of 9 to 16 or so, before he got really tied up with baseball and other athletics," Myron says. "This would have been between 1958 and 1967 or so when my brother Donald was in the Navy. So Leo would help with the farm chores — feeding the cows and doing a little bit of milking."

When Leo first came to the farm, cows were something new to him, as he had never been close enough to touch one. At the time, Myron's family had about 50 head of dairy cattle, including milk cows, calves and heifers.

"Leo was a big-boned kid, but never fat," Myron says. "He carried his weight well and he worked hard at the farm chores. He had a thing for cows — he was very enthused in feeding them and talking to them. It was really something to see because Leo loved those animals."

Chet Golembiewski, Leo's younger brother by 11 months, remembers the two of them playing hockey on the river in Illinois.

"We'd walk down Plainfield Road to the river when we were kids — it was about a mile from our house," Chet says. "It had to be below zero or the river wouldn't be frozen. When it was frozen, we'd slip past Reno's Gas Station and use boards and two-by-fours to clear off the ice so we could skate."

Of the two Golembiewski boys, Leo was the natural skater.

"I was a pretty good shooter, but my skating was marginal," Chet says. "I was always into rebounding where I'd bounce it off the goalie and see where it goes. Leo always was very good at stopping the shots."

Chet believes that the most important thing he learned from Leo was what Chet calls "stick-to-it-tiveness," a sense that once you start something, you finish it.

"He showed it to me when we played hockey, where if you stick to it, you'll eventually get it done," Chet says. "And I learned to use it, so when we played baseball, I wasn't as good as him because he was so much more focused, but I could hit him when he pitched, and nobody else could."

Chet says both he and Leo hit the ball very hard, learning to develop such a hard swing that if the hit was a grounder, it was very difficult to catch.

"On the other hand, we both had our share of strikeouts, but also home runs and hits," he adds.

Losing wasn't one of the parts of baseball or hockey that Leo tolerated, Chet remembers.

"Leo would really be upset when he lost," Chet says. "I would be upset for awhile and then would find something else to do, working on go carts or cars because I was a motorhead. For Leo, losing was upsetting because he put all of his free time into sports."

Elementary school is where the Golembiewski boys honed their baseball skills. After running their paper routes on Saturdays, they would meet other kids at Lincoln Elementary School in Brookfield, Illinois, and if there were enough gloves, played hard ball.

"If there weren't enough gloves, we'd play mushball or softball where we had to catch with our bare hands," Chet says. "We all loved playing ball, whether practice or an actual game. We'd play before school started, during lunch, and then after school. It was how we grew up in blue-collar Lyons, Illinois, but

I never took the game as seriously as Leo did."

Chet thinks his brother still is a little too serious when it comes to life.

"Leo can come off as very funny because he has a great sense of humor, but overall he can get much too serious about things," Chet says. "He's always been that way, yet he can be a very funny guy when he wants to."

Still, Chet says he couldn't think of having a cooler brother when growing up.

"He always kept an eye on me because both of our parents worked," Chet says. "So I always looked up to Leo."

Leo was the first person from the Golembiewski family to attend college, something the entire family continues to be proud of, Chet says.

"Leo's best quality is love," Chet points out. "He loves in a way that's difficult for some people to see, but his generosity and love of others are incredible."

Sometimes Leo's seriousness gets the better of him.

"When Leo gets upset, his temper undoes him," Chet says. "He's like a teddy bear because he's such a good person and so generous, but when he goes off, people could get the wrong impression of him if they don't know him very well. When you put all of Leo's pieces together, he's quite incredible."

Paula Golembiewski has been married to Leo since October 15, 1977 and believes that most people perceive him differently than he really is.

"Leo comes across as a gruff, tough guy, but he's a very gentle person," Paula says. "He's not the tough guy he portrays — he's really a softie at heart. He's a soft touch for kids and animals."

While Leo and Paula don't have any children, they do have cats and have had dogs and tortoises, and Leo has certainly helped raise many young people.

"Leo has always had dogs and cats in his life, back to when he was growing up," Paula says. "When he was coaching high school hockey in La-Grange, Illinois, at the end of the season his first high school team bought him a duck and called it 'Scotty Roberts,' nicknamed 'Quack.'"

At the time, Leo had a collie named Laddie, Paula says. It wasn't unusual for the duck and Laddie to walk down the street together, stopping traffic along the way, the collie leading, followed by the duck.

"Leo is such a sucker for animals," Paula observes.

Paula also sees Leo's sense of humor more frequently than most people.

"He takes a lot of things seriously, but his sense of humor is just bubbling under the surface," she says. "It's there, but the public doesn't see it very much, but when Leo lets his hair down, it really comes out."

Leo usually doesn't bring his work home with him, although he sometimes will seek Paula's opinion about how the Icecats team played a particular game.

"He might ask me what I thought and I'll give my opinion, but it doesn't happen all that often," Paula says. "His mind is always working where he's thinking about what can be done to improve the team. He's definitely a problem solver."

Paula is a much more low-key individual than Leo and doesn't get "as worked up over some things like he does," she says. "I try to get him to relax and look at situations from different angles instead of approaching them from only a single direction. I like to suggest alternative views and he always listens."

But what about that hard guy exterior?

"That's the way he's made himself because he wants to appear as the tough guy, but he really isn't," she says. "He'll always keep that image because it shows he's confident in his own skin, but once you get to know him, you can see he's not as unapproachable as he appears — he's actually a gentle, great guy."

4.
The Road to Hockey Coach

When I was ten years old, I thought that goaltending was the most important spot on a hockey team, maybe as much as the first baseman or pitcher is in baseball, which is what made the goalie position attractive to me so that's where I wanted to play. By the time I was 11 years old I had already begun idolizing Glenn Hall. That's when it all started for me.

Before that age, I wasn't even skating because there were no skates to be had in my family. They were too expensive. I finally got an old pair of skates and I remember being on my neighbor's frozen driveway, trying to stand up, then skating in between cars and catching car door handles before falling.

So there I was, playing pickup hockey games, and I was the goalie with non-goalie skates. Goalie skates have a longer, thicker blade and are much flatter. That way, you can use them almost as a stick and to make saves.

I really began to get serious about playing hockey when I reached high school. I did not play any organized hockey until I went to college. My family and I simply couldn't afford it. I would walk over to the Des Plaines River in Lyons, Illinois, with skates and pads over my shoulder, or I would sling the skates over the handlebars and ride my bike along 47th Street to McCook, Illinois, almost getting killed every time because of trucks going by at night. It was a very heavily traveled road, but we would ride our bikes on it, even during the winter.

There was no high school hockey back then, so we played pickup games and some semi-organized hockey against a men's league. I was used to playing with older players because I had always played with the older kids from the neighborhoods. At the time, I was the 12 year old goalie who could take it from the big guys. I was this crazy kid who would goalie against anybody.

For our pickup games and with the men's leagues, we played on outside rinks in Illinois — in Hinsdale, and in Lombard on the Des Plaines River. We even skated on flooded parking lots if that was all that was available to us. So it was when I was in the seventh grade when I started playing tons of hockey outside in all kinds of weather.

I always played goal because that was my position and nobody ever wanted to be the goalie. No one wanted to stand in front of the puck. So I used to get picked up by the guys from the Lyons Post Office team to play with them. These were guys who were in their 20s and 30s and I was only 13 years old. They would come by my house on Sunday mornings after mass and we'd go skate and play hockey.

I also remember that the kind of gear we had was primitive. We had pads to wear, but I didn't have any goalie pads until I got to college. I did wear a mask. One time when I had forgotten to bring my mask and played without it, I got popped and lost a front tooth. The mask that I had back then was nothing like the ones that goalies have today.

During high school, we would get a group of guys together and play pickup games. At that time, it was mostly still outside, but sometimes, very rarely, a bunch of us friends would rent ice to play on. Later, when I was in college, we rented ice much more frequently.

When I decided on a college, hockey didn't have that much of an influence on my decision. I decided to go to my high school, St. Procopius Academy, now Benet Academy in Lisle, Illinois, with the intent of eventually becoming a Benedictine monk. St. Procopius was a Benedictine high school, which also had a Benedictine college called St. Procopius College. It's now named Benedictine University.

The coach and hockey team at St. Procopius College knew that I was going to attend there, a freshman goalie coming to them from Benet High School. The high school and college were literally across the street from each other. I knew that I could have a college career, and once I got there, the goalie job was mine to lose. I didn't lose it. In fact I was able to play every game in each season, the four years that I was in college.

Our record the first three years I played goalie was terrible. Our first year we won 3 and lost 12. My sophomore year, we won 3, lost 13 and with 3 ties. When I was a junior, we won 4 and lost 12. I led the league in saves every year. I averaged 50 saves of shots on goal a game. You have to remember that a shot on goal is on a 6 foot by 4 foot space, which is the net. The shot has to be on the net in order for it to be considered a shot on goal.

In my senior year we picked up a couple of forwards from the Chicago Catholic league and were able to post a 13 wins and 6 losses record. We went on to win the Midwest Collegiate Hockey League championship. I was still averaging a lot of saves per game; that didn't change.

I even had two shutouts that year, which was a neat vindication for me. We played an undefeated team, Northern Illinois University, and beat them 6 to 0. The next night we beat Lewis University for the championship. We actually went from last to first place.

After games when I was in college, and also during the summer, we would go up to the Polar Dome in Dundee and play on Sunday nights in the men's league to get more ice time. Not everyone on my college hockey team did that, but the core of the players did.

I was supposed to enter the monastery after my sophomore year in college. The way it worked was you would become a novice for the first year at St. Procopius Abbey. This would be a year away from the world where you lived in a monastery and if they accepted you, you professed, and would go back to college, across the street, and finish your junior and senior year. Once that was accomplished, you would go off to the seminary to take your classes to become a priest.

In the spring of my sophomore year, I made my decision and told Abbot Daniel Kucera, O.S.B. that I wanted to finish my college education and continue with my hockey. I think his reaction was that we all have free will to make choices. As for myself, I didn't have time to be disappointed with my choice because as it turned out, with my best friend Bob Mackey got killed in an automobile accident on July 31, 1969, this was the event that changed my life.

That summer I worked six days a week, 12 hours a day in a factory in Chicago, the Litho Strip at 48th and Kilborne. The company made gigantic sheet metal and plastics. I hated the work thoroughly. I worked from 8 at night to 8 in the morning, six days a week. I still wanted to be involved with baseball and was coaching Babe Ruth baseball, so essentially I lived on next to no sleep for about a dozen weeks during that summer.

It was a pivot point in my life the year Bob Mackey got killed. For the first time in my life, I applied my faith, belief in humanity and desire to help people. I quit the Litho Strip job immediately after Bob's death. His girlfriend took his death very badly; she was 17 years old and terribly distraught. She didn't want to go on and I had to help her move away from those kinds of thoughts.

I returned home from a trip to New Brunswick, Canada on the day of the lunar landing, July 20, and 11 days later Bob was dead, leaving a big scar in my life. During the previous two weeks at a hockey camp in Canada, recommended to me by my idol, Glenn Hall, who was in his second year with the St. Louis Blues in 1969, is where I first met Scotty Bowman, coach of the St. Louis

Blues, Danny Grant, a 50 goal scorer at the time, and Claude LaRose of the Montreal Canadiens. Those guys shot at me for two weeks as I was taught by NHL Hall of Famer Jacques Plante.

I met Glenn Hall one-on-one for the first time on December 8, 1965, when I was a junior in high school, and we have been buddies ever since. I had sent a letter to Billy Reay, the coach of the Chicago Black Hawks and the winningest coach in the National Hockey League at the time, saying I wanted to meet Glenn Hall, and he arranged it.

I would pal around and go to Black Hawks games to see Glenn after the games. I even got to know his wife Pauline. Glenn told me about the camp that was something new that Scotty Bowman would attend, along with other NHL professional players — guys like Jacques Plante. Besides the hockey, one of my strongest memories is of eating peanut butter and jelly sandwiches with Jacques Plante every day in between workouts.

The two week hockey camp in Canada was for players 18 and under and we were categorized by age. I flew to Canada, the first time I ever flew in an airplane. My first leg was a jet plane to Toronto, then a smaller plane to Montreal, and finally a four-prop plane to St. John, New Brunswick. The camp was taught by Plante and we got to do a lot of work on the ice. I had a chance to spend time with guys who I watched play in Chicago Stadium and there I was on the ice, skating with them. This was a dream come true for me.

I also got the chance to get shot at by NHL players for the first time. I remember the first shot that Danny Grant took at me. I had a better chance of seeing God than of touching the puck, but after awhile I got better at touching the puck.

I attended the Pro Camp with the St. Louis Blues in Flint, Michigan in September 1971, at the invitation of the late NHL Hall of Famer Lynn Patrick. Attending the Pro Camp is by invitation only. I wasn't a free agent, but I was invited as a non-roster player. I had graduated from college in May of 1971.

The St. Louis Blues training camp went on up to the start of the National Hockey League regular season. I was one of their goalies. The goalies at the camp with NHL experience were Jacques Caron, Ernie Wakely, Jim McLeod, Peter McDuffe and Chris Worthy. The remaining goalies were second round draft pick John Garrett, Grant Cole and me. I had a decent 2.6 goals against average during the time I was there.

After one week, I was on the Kansas City Blues roster to start during that week of scrimmages. This was the St. Louis Blues minor league team. When I got a shutout on the third day, I was put on the St. Louis Blues roster. On the fifth day, I started the game for the Blues, and I gave up four or five goals. I don't remember much about that game. As the camp continued, later in the week I went back to Chicago, being told, "We'll find a place to put you."

I didn't go and play in the International League as the Blues had suggested because my dad was in the hospital. My brother Chet had put me through college, but I didn't know that until I was 28 years old. The International League was a minor league. I didn't take it on because I couldn't afford to play for $200 bucks a week. Instead, I got a job in a factory in the production office and kept in shape, skating a lot, but for no apparent reason.

In March of 1972, I went to St. Louis with my equipment and skated with the St. Louis Blues. Sid Abel, Hall of Famer and general manager at the time, told me I should come on down and attend a rookie camp at the Arena in September of 1972. They were going to have six goalies from across the country there, along with forwards and defensemen.

At the beginning, the incoming rookie players were almost arrested by the US Secret Service because of a big Democrat political thing going on at the Arena, with Democratic Presidential nominee George McGovern in attendance. As the limo pulled up I tried to shake McGovern's hand and was surrounded by a herd of agents. We were lucky that we had St. Louis Blues ID's because it could have been ugly.

During the St. Louis Blues camp there were two games, the first against the St. Louis University Billikins, a NCAA Division I team. Our team was known as the St. Louis Blues Rookie team. The next game would be against the St. Louis Blues Amateur All Stars.

I was wearing Jacque Plante's number 30 and I started the game against the All Stars. I remember stepping on the ice and it was like a magical moment. We won the game and I had a shutout. I signed autographs while another goalie played the second half of the game. People loved Leo from Chicago, which was my nickname with the St. Louis Blues players, as well as Sid Salomon III, the owner of the Blues.

The camp that culminated with those two exhibition games had top players. On my team were Bernie Doan, a defenseman whose son is Shane Doan of the Phoenix Coyotes and Pierre Dupont, who played with the Philadelphia Flyers.

I went back home and Lynn Patrick called a couple of times, trying to work out something for me to go to the Eastern League to play hockey. I was in Illinois about a week and a half and got a coaching job at Lyons Township High School in LaGrange, Illinois as their first varsity hockey coach. I already had coached baseball four or five years and wanted to give back to the American players what I had learned from Jimmy Roberts, Lynn Patrick, Scotty Bowman, Glenn Hall and many others.

That was my entrance into coaching hockey and I wound up being the epitome of how Scotty Bowman coached, which is why my wife Paula wanted me to change back to the way I used to coach the past few years. The players and times have changed and you can't coach like you did in the old days. But while technique has changed, philosophy hasn't.

I may be an ex-goalie, but there are not too many college hockey coaches who have a master's degree in education. I spent a lot of years in the classroom and I know kids better than they think. A couple of cups of coffee with the Blues organization over four years didn't hurt either.

I started coaching baseball when I was in college, in a Babe Ruth league in Brookfield, Illinois. I tagged along and before I knew it I got added to the coaching staff.

I played baseball my freshman year in college, lettering that year. A new coach was hired my sophomore year and he didn't want me to play hockey anymore, so I had to choose between hockey and baseball. I ultimately chose hockey. At the time, I played first base and pitched. Baseball always has been my passion; hockey, my job.

I coached baseball through my college years, through the mid 1970s and close to the time when I left Illinois in 1979 to move to Arizona. In Chicago, I coached both baseball and hockey at the same time. In Tucson I coached baseball at Salpointe Catholic High School, as well as the Arizona Icecats and baseball at the Pony League level and at Sabino High School.

Coaching is all about teaching kids. Hockey is the vehicle that I use now; baseball was the vehicle that was most important then. As an educator, and I always look at it from that slant, my prime motivation is trying to help raise these kids the right way.

Coaching these days, I sometimes have trouble with older players who want to infiltrate the younger players, because I'm not in favor of drinking or doing drugs. When the right woman comes along, they will know, but when you're an undergrad, trying to find out who your are, where you want to go and what you want to be, you don't need to be tied down to peers and others telling you what to do as you try to find out who you are and what life is about.

When I was a high school hockey coach in Illinois, I had a pretty good record. I won 300 games and lost 40 in seven years. One year we were 61-1-1.

But the things that I told the high school kids, I can't say to college kids. I don't want these kids to lose a game for me to prove that I'm right.

I'm a very philosophical guy and sort of religious, but I'm also a tough act guy. I didn't go to law school because I wasn't going to wear a suit and tie six days a week and take a train downtown. People ask me why I wear jeans and tee shirts most the time, even now when I've gotten older. It's simply my style and desired everyday appearance.

The bottom line is that I try to get the most out of my players and I try to get the most out of my years of experience and education. You can use a partner in life's journey.

5.
Motivation

Motivating players during a game or practice is something that I've never had trouble with. Whether you're winning or losing a game, how you get to that point will determine the prime factor in what you have to say to the players, in what you have to do to motivate them. If the team is working hard in practice, if it's been focused, then I'm more apt to talk about what they've specifically done wrong on the ice, whether it be back checking, fore checking or passing — what I do is give them the actual "here's what we have to do to get the job done. We know you're focused mentally, but here's what we're not doing on the ice."

When you have a situation where the team isn't focused, which automatically will hurt with their execution, to almost have to use the back door on them. What I try to do is get them to understand how they get to a certain point mentally; that is, the point which is depriving us of executing properly. Once they make that connection, they can see where they have to be to execute well. So motivation depends on the given situation at hand. Focus determines reality.

Starting the season out strong is the essence of making Nationals. In 2007-2008, with a record of 22-8-1, we didn't qualify for Nationals, though we lost only a couple of times in the second half of the season. I attribute that to a lack of focus because of their lifestyle. I almost have to talk to the team in the context of their lifestyle, the Arizona lifestyle. The team morale is great because the players are in love with the "Arizona" lifestyle. They come to play for the Arizona Icecats and then they fall in love with the Arizona lifestyle. The University of Arizona has a great campus and there's great weather in Tucson pretty much year round. The players are living in their condos, the weather is great and everything is just a dreamland compared to what they've experienced anywhere else. Looking at it from a coach's point of view, that lifestyle is a distraction, absolutely, and that can be a concern.

Our number one scorer that year, who got hurt and had to sit out the rest of the year, gave me a solid explanation of why he thought we were 13 and 10 at that point. Without an inkling, he said, "goaltending," and he was right.

You can't win games and be a successful team without solid goaltending. Unless you score 8 goals and only give up 7, you won't win hockey games.

What I say to motivate a team depends on the given predicament that the team finds itself in. For the past 39 years I've said that hockey is 75 percent mental. You're skating at 35 miles an hour, and the puck is flying around at 100 miles an hour, players have to be very attentive to the skill factor of the game. A player's skill level absolutely will go up or down depending on how prepared mentally he is for the game or the practice.

Scotty Bowman, a mentor of mine, used to say, "Mental preparation is the key to success and execution." Today's hockey players — well, some don't agree and some don't understand it.

The key to motivation is mental preparation. A player has to prepare himself for practice. He has to get into the locker room 15 or 20 minutes early and shouldn't be thinking about what he just saw in the mall or the homework that he has to do tonight, or his girlfriend, or the fight he had with mom and dad. He has to prepare himself to execute and hone his skills.

Each player has to be treated differently. I'm a huge believer in self motivation, self esteem and self respect. Often your best people in a particular area lack self esteem in their daily lives. It's the persona they bring to their jobs that gets them through that — who they really are, who they'd really like to be.

I'm a classic example of that. I've never had self esteem. But I want to build these kids up so they feel good about themselves. Some teams have almost cartoon like characters. There's a Daffy Duck type guy or a Mickey Mouse player who show their lack of even wanting to care. The fact that they don't want to show this stuff means something to them because it's not cool to care about anything.

The way I've tried to coach is to develop the player as a whole person, someone for whom hockey is a vehicle and not the answer to all his problems. I want hockey to help the player find out who he is or where he wants to go by his actions, discipline, dedication, sacrifice, responsibility and commitment. From hockey those elements carry over to the more important things in a person's life — the studying, the relationships with parents and relationships with friends and acquaintances. In many cases, that's what my job is. I'm an educator first. Winning hockey games is the byproduct of doing a good job.

That's when I have a tendency to be more critical — when we're winning. That's when I'm doing the nitpicking and dealing with the little things. When we're losing, I try to be more supportive.

I sometimes like to go after the intangibles more than anything else. The players can see what they're doing wrong physically, whether it be a lack of execution or passing or shooting, but at times you have to pick them up by the bootstraps psychologically and tell them, in a caring way, that we can go beyond what they're doing or we can do better.

If you want to win a national championship, you've must have great goaltending. When we won the national championship in 1985, and those times when we went to the final four, or where we were runner up, the goaltending was great, the defense was good and the offense was consistent.

The Icecats have only had two losing seasons in all these years. I've never had a losing season when I was a high school coach. Out of the 32 years of coaching the Icecats, I only had two seasons where the losses were bigger than the wins — an 11-14-1 season few years ago and another one at 12-18-0.

Losing and winning are both determined by the coaches and players, plus the job they have done together. Give your best and work hard; that's the key to success. The four-letter word that I try to teach my players, and we go after that immediately, is you want them to CARE. That's the word that means the most to this coach.

In high school the kids don't understand that concept. Socio-economically they're in great shape because they have everything under the sun they might want. They have good parental units and strong family backgrounds. Or perhaps the parents are fighting who they are, what they want to be, and what they wish they could be. So the task is in getting the kids to care about a sport over and beyond their own particular needs or desires.

The higher level you get in any organized sports, whether a college or pro team, then the more likely you will have more players with more personal issues to deal with. But somewhere along the line, the team will care — either about their coaches, their teammates, getting the job done and winning the game, their execution, or the execution of their teammates.

Our players go back and look at the early Arizona Icecats teams, and what they did and how they did it. These guys today are playing for the University of Arizona Icecats in a 7,000 seat arena and they view it as their right to play in the "Madhouse on Main Street," forgetting that it should be viewed as a privilege. It's the tail wagging the dog, so to speak, but having founded the program, and after 32 years, I feel that I've seen and done it all.

My philosophy of teaching, coaching and mentoring hasn't changed. The modus operandi has to change because the kids are different than they were years ago. You can't shoot fire and brimstone at kids today unless the players understand teamwork, hard work and caring are the keys to overall success, which is difficult to achieve.

31

Caring for your team and your teammates, and being successful, has to come from the heart and from the soul. It happens to be part of the very fiber of who you are.

A lot of kids today don't know who they are because of the tremendous pressure from their parents, their peers, from music and entertainment. These kids are really not sure about life. There are all sorts of underlying pressures pulling them in completely different directions. When I was 18, I knew everything, like them, but the older you get, the less you know. That's what the players call a Coach G-ism.

When I was a kid, I never smoked, drank or tried marijuana, and have not done so to this day. I didn't swear like a lot of the other kids did. On Saturday night, the Blackhawks were televised on station WGN so we'd go down to a friend's basement where he had a net painted on the wall in black paint. Me and a few other guys, were shooting real pucks in the basement at that net from about 10 to 12 feet away. We'd do that before the game and in between periods. For us, it was a wild Saturday night when we were growing up. On the other hand, I can only remember bowling about two or three times because we didn't have money to spend on bowling. The world has completely changed. Those days, we didn't have any money. The world is not such a very nice place now. Coaching is very, very difficult, compared to how it used to be.

I've always thought of myself as the keeper of the zoo. When we were playing at Penn State for a national championship before they had tiebreakers, we tied all 3 games, which eliminated us from the national championship. This is the team we had with Kelly Walker, the Icecats all time leading scorer with 81 points that season.

At the time, we were on a cold, school bus, being shuttled from the hotel to the Penn State arena. Now I'm a very colorful guy, but what was really funny was that Kelly Walker stood up in front of everybody with a pair of gloves on his hands. Kelly was a big knucklehead, but was one of the best hockey players we ever had. He got up and did an oration where he raised his clenched fist and talked about the coach, who was not only the keeper of the zoo, but now actually a member of the zoo. That was the best award that I ever got and it was even more special because it came from a player.

When things like that happen, it makes you feel as if you've actually got to the players. At that point, for whatever small point in time, those kids understood who you really are. Right now I'm just the keeper of the zoo again. But back then, according to the team, I was made a member with them.

There have been people who have called me a madman because I'm not afraid to let my players be flamboyant and I say things that motivates them.

The important thing is that my players know that I'd climb a mountain for them.

Here are a couple more Coach G-isms that I use with the players.

- Life's a climb — It's worth the view.
- Be the best college hockey player you can, first. Then go after being a pro.
- And one from Bob Newhart on a piece about Abraham Lincoln — You don't quit being a lawyer to be a rail-splitter.
- I walk on water only when it's frozen.
- If we lose, it's the coach's fault; if we win, the victory is the team's.
- Oh yeah — if you play a sport, go ahead!

6.
Life and Abraham Lincoln

Today is Ash Wednesday, so I'm eating tuna fish sandwiches for lunch. In the Roman Catholic religion, Ash Wednesday begins the season of Lent and Catholics don't eat meat on that day or on Fridays during Lent. One of the things about being a Catholic and having spent six years studying for the priesthood, is that it tends to make you reflective. In reflecting back over my life, it's been a very interesting 32 years I've invested in the Icecats. I think the thing that makes me reflective and even grateful is that this has been my life's work. I started out on this career when I was 29 years old, and now I'm 61.

There's not much you can do either way to affect the way people perceive you and what you've done. The Arizona Icecats and Leo Golembiewski will most likely be remembered long after the Icecats are gone and long after I'm gone. What we did together over those 30 years will not be forgotten. I've mused about what former US President George W. Bush worried about what history would say about him. It's interesting that President Richard Nixon was of a similar mind, worrying about how history would cast him and his legacy, but our most popular and recognizable president, Abraham Lincoln didn't concern himself with his legacy.

What I admire about Abraham Lincoln is the fact that the guy was a self made man. He was born in backwoods Kentucky, spent a little time in Indiana and finally got to Illinois. He was a self taught lawyer for the most part, and ultimately a powerful railroad lawyer who had a lot of nerve, a lot of inner strength and at the same time was a pretty religious guy in an unorthodox way, although not in the conventional sense.

Lincoln was self effacing in his humor. I'm probably more like that, although my image is more of a tough guy who's got it together. I can tell you that's a fabrication — it's the image that I have to portray because nobody is going to follow unless they think you're introspective and reflective. The biggest thing to learn about Abraham Lincoln is in how he handled himself. He had a lot of demons to deal with, but he was able to over come them. There are a lot of demons in my life too.

Life has a purpose. What strikes home with me, especially in the last five years or so, is that in your 20s, 30s and 40s, you're too busy surviving to notice what's going on, but later in life, you get more reflective. You start getting emails from people who you coached in high school or college, and they are thanking you.

I got a call one day from Glenn Hall's wife. Glenn was out ice fishing, Pauline was listening to Rex Allen Jr. and the Sons of the Pioneers music. She and Glenn had met them through me when they were in Tucson, so listening to the songs triggered a memory, and she thought of the coach and gave me a call.

The interesting thing about life is that you never think about people thinking of you. Somehow, it doesn't occur to you to think that you're in their thoughts. I can honestly say that I've never thought that people would think about me and when it happens I've always been kind of surprised.

I always want 100 percent success in dealing with my friends and those whom I'm in contact with. This book focuses not only on the Icecats winning ways, but more on my prime philosophy as a teacher, coach, mentor and educator. I've always tried to dedicate my life to helping people, but as Abraham Lincoln said, "You can't please all of the people all of the time."

On the other hand, I can be my worst enemy. Nobody beats me up more than I do. I've often thought about what the Benedictines would say about that. My answer always is that they'd tell me to "lighten up." Because I know myself so well, I know that I won't.

During the 39 years I've been dealing with kids from ages 13 to 25, I've learned that it's almost not so much they don't want to be helped, but they don't know how to be helped. So I've tried to show them the way, to get to them.

You can consider life like a hockey practice. As a coach, (and even for the players themselves), we set forth goals for a given practice. We try to do drills and the kind of things that get the most out of the players physically and mentally without them knowing that we're doing it.

I might tell my players, "Okay, we're going to do 20 line sprints at the end of every practice. All you got to do is up and back 20 times. That's the bad part of practice because all you're doing is having to skate."

Rather than do 20 line sprints at the end of every practice, what I do is I structure the practices in such a way that they're doing those sprints, even ten times that number of sprints, during the practice, without noticing them. So the players get the work done, and they're not realizing that they're moving their legs or shooting the puck. It's simply like a magician's misdirection in how we execute it.

I have used "bread and butter" drills — constant repetition of skating, shooting, passing and puck handling — like Scotty Bowman and Jimmy Roberts did. You get to know all the facets of your game that way.

Sometimes I think it's too bad that youth is wasted on young people. Since I started coaching at the high school level, I always believed, and preached to the kids, that the sooner you get to know who you are, the better. So I try to treat these kids as peers. I may be the coach, but I can learn things from them too.

However, I do set the rules when it comes to the context of drinking, smoking and certain types of language, but I try to make the players feel they also play an important part in the relationship. That's part of what I set to do for all these years, and friendship has a part in it, without a doubt.

Part of it has to do with philosophy, what you bring to the table with the people whom you deal with. If all I'm concerned with is only the wins we post, then I'm not fulfilling my responsibilities as an educator. I wouldn't be fulfilling my responsibilities as a mentor. So winning a hockey game is one of the results of getting the most out of the players. You'll find that hard work, discipline, commitment and a lot of intangibles become the vehicle that works for those kids.

When I think about not being actively involved in education any more, I regret that I had to leave Salpointe Catholic High School. I enjoyed teaching there immensely, from 1979 until 1985, especially the American government class.

In looking back over the years, I think that people in general, and kids specifically, changed after the deaths of John F. Kennedy, Martin Luther King Jr. and Bobby Kennedy. The Beatles brought long hair to the United States and the American culture in 1964. Not long after that, people changed during and after the Vietnam War. I see it as the destruction of the family and the rise of the drug culture. It didn't affect how I taught because I wasn't teaching then, surrounded by the changing culture and society.

However, I can say it absolutely affected me. When it came time in June of 1969 for me to make a decision on whether or not to join a monastery for my novitiate year, I knew in my heart that I wanted to finish my hockey career at Benedictine University (St. Procopius College) first. When I knew I wanted to be a Benedictine, it was because they were both teachers and coaches — two endeavors that I highly aspired to. The Benedictines taught me a lot about academics, and what they accomplished as a monastic community. Initially, I felt that I didn't want to join the monastery because of my hockey interest, but by the time I graduated from college in 1971 and pursued hockey, I realized the best I could do would be to teach and get to the kids as a lay person. At that point, I would say my decision changed the direction of my life.

Would I go back and change that direction in my life? I don't think so, mainly because of the significance of my wife, Paula, on my life. Looking back, I wouldn't change a thing in that regard. The only thing I regret, that I wish I could have done in my life, is change water and bread into the blood and body of Christ as a priest in saying Mass.

In terms of people, I always have viewed friendships as something that's vitally important in life. If I have any regrets in my life, it might be the religious thing, that I never could serve God as a priest, followed by not having played a regular season game in the National Hockey League nor having been a coach in the NHL, though I had opportunities to do so.

Whenever there's something that we regret in life, we can usually find something better to balance it out. For me, I found someone who took me for what I was and found out the good, bad and ugly in Leo Golembiewski. Paula and I have been married 33 years and I'm proud of our love and life together more than anything.

With Bob Mackey's death, I can still see in my mind's eye, him laying in the casket, having been broadsided by another car, and all the bones in his body broken. At such a time, you learn that life is fragile and that you're not immortal. When you're 18 or 19 the last thing you think about is your mortality, which is the problem with kids and many of my players today.

You have to live life to the fullest and don't take yourself out of the game. Don't be reckless, because you're young and only live once.

Life, indeed, is so fragile. For a lot of kids, their first incidence of death is a grandparent being lost. I only knew one of my grandparents — my paternal grandmother died when I was ten. The Golembiewski's had 13 siblings on dad's side, so you learn about your mortality pretty quickly.

In response to Bob Mackey's death, I bought a life insurance policy that summer. I figured that if anything happened to me, the insurance policy would help my mom and dad.

Once again, part of my philosophy of life is that you should live your life to the fullest and live each day like it will be your last. I don't mean that morbidly, but you should live like you might not be here tomorrow.

It's a tough world out there these days, something that I see every day as I coach these college players. I can honestly say that I wouldn't want to be a teenager again. Look at all the distractions and temptations these kids have today. Doing it once is enough, like "Twilight Zone, the Movie" in the Scatman Crothers scene at the old people's home — nobody wanted to be 18 again.

I regret and simultaneously don't regret the fact that I really never had a childhood because I was supposed to be the family priest. My childhood consisted of playing baseball and playing hockey. These days, baseball is my passion and hockey is my job. During my childhood, both were of equal importance to me. Yet with the craziness that other kids showed in how they acted out, I felt that I had to be more proper. I didn't get into trouble. I was God-fearing enough.

In these times, I really don't think that a lot of kids realize there is a God. I don't think they're non-believers, but for them, God is simply somewhere or someone out there and just another concept. God is not something that's a part of their everyday lives.

Some of that non-belief or non-acceptance makes my style of coaching so hard on me. If I don't reach people, really get to them, then I think that I've failed. That's my honest belief.

In order to have been as successful as I've been, I've had to reach a majority of players during each hockey season. Even though I think that the record doesn't mean much in any given year, still, it's an indicator of the program's success. If you want to take the long look at the situation, it's the University's program too, all players being full-time undergrads. It's the fans, and my fans are the real thing, who help make the team successful.

I feel that you have to try to get the most out of your players and get them to buy into you, even if it's 25 percent here and 33 percent there. It doesn't always have to be 100 percent, all of the time. Otherwise, you're not going to win 75 percent of your games consistently year in and out for 30 years as we have done. For 32 years the program has brought 30 to 50 out of state tuitions to the University's coffers, which made a lot of money for them.

One of the maxims I work by is that we have to work harder than anyone else. I'm not trying to sell myself on these kids. Rather, I want them to take each game the same way. Every game they play should be a tough game. My players know they should approach every game as a tough game. One year we lost 8 of our 14 losses by a single goal. Ouch — that was a tough season. Some people say you can be an ordinary coach and say the players blew the game and the season, but I'm an educator and a mentor and I don't believe in that philosophy. We shouldn't be in the game for the victories. The victories will be the byproduct of how well you perform, how well you execute. If you don't win there are a lot of ramifications to consider.

Whether I'm in the locker room, on the ice, in the classroom or talking with friends and neighbors, I call a spade a spade. I have this rough, tough guy exterior because if I didn't I would have been trampled years ago. For me it's simply a matter of survival. I'm not a conflict person by any stretch of the imagination, but like to think I'm as real and an everyday person as anyone else. I choose substance over fame.

I also like to think of this book as a story that fits every coach or wannabe coach in the country, because it comes from the heart and deals with the basic elements of helping make players see their potential. Maybe, if I write a second book, it will be titled, "I Only Walk on Water When It's Frozen."

7.
Deciding on the Desert

Paula and I often visited Tucson during the Easter school break and eventually made the decision to move to the desert in the fall of 1979 to start a college hockey team of American-born players. It was a difficult thing for Paula and I to do because we came to Tucson with debt from Chicago. Back there, I coached high school hockey at Lyons Township and at the same time, for four years, ran the Chalet Sports Core ice rink in Willow Springs, Illinois. Paula was working downtown at the Chicago Mercantile Exchange. We both had good jobs there, but needed a bill-paying job in Tucson. As it happened, I came out to Tucson in August to start teaching at Salpointe Catholic High School and Paula came out that October.

When I arrived in Tucson, I went to Salpointe and got an appointment with Father Frank McCarthy, who then was the principal of the school. I told him a little bit about the crazy idea I had for a desert hockey team, and then a lot more about my background with the Benedictines and the priesthood, as well as my teaching and coaching history. I was fortunate that he hired me to teach religion for the start of the 1979-80 school year.

I had to go back to Chicago for a brief time because the Chalet Sports Core was being transitioned into a sports fitness complex that included racquetball courts and swimming pools, so the timing for me to leave Chicago and that job was right. Paula and I didn't have any house to sell because we were living in the house my brother Chet and I grew up in. When my brother got married in 1975 and moved to Downers Grove, Illinois, I was the one who took care of the house.

The transition from Chicago to Tucson was an easy one for me because it was something we had planned for a long time. We both knew the change was coming and looked forward to it. I had fallen in love with Tucson when I drove my parents out here in 1972, which is where they retired. I became totally enamored of the desert and the mountains surrounding the city. Probably the only thing missing for me was the Chicago White Sox because baseball has always been my passion, and particularly the White Sox.

I don't think I missed the big city feel of Chicago as much as I thought I might. These days, I like to get back to Chicago to experience that big-city feeling two or three times a year, and use the opportunities mostly for recruiting players or visiting with family or sometimes simply because the White Sox are playing in town. I still can picture myself driving north on the Stevenson Expressway with downtown on my left in the distance — the Sears Tower and Hancock Center reaching for the sky. Every time I look at that scene, it's almost like when I've looked at the Grand Canyon — every time I'm awed by the view.

I think I miss Tucson more now when I go to Chicago because I miss the vastness of the desert. Considering how far it was from our house in Lyons to the Benedictines at St. Procopius and from our house here on the east side of Tucson to midtown, one realizes how much is scrunched into 12 miles back in Chicago. I may miss it at times, but I'm not pining away for it. It was a great place to grow up, in the suburbs. I always liked the feel of being in Lyons, which was on the edge of nothing. Travel 45 minutes the other way and you can be on the Chicago lakefront.

As I said, we had decided to move to Tucson in 1975, come hell or high water. Paula hated the idea of moving from the beginning. Besides, Pope John Paul II was scheduled to come to Chicago in early October 1979 and we had tickets to see him at Five Holy Martyrs Parish. Paula and I agreed that I would come to Tucson in August to begin teaching and laying the hands on groundwork for the Icecats at the U of A. We planned a lot of the groundwork we needed to do, starting in the summer of 1977.

In October, I flew to Chicago to see the pope and Paula and I drove back to Tucson together the first week of October. For me the move was no big deal — it went very smoothly. I had my mind and my dream in place. I had the goal of getting this whole thing going and now I was actually doing it.

Because we were becoming the Ice Hockey club for the University of Arizona, we had to go through a lot of paperwork to get accredited by the Associate Students of the University of Arizona. Besides all the paperwork, I was busy meeting prospective hockey players, even though I already had a few players who had come out to Tucson right away.

The first actual practice for the Icecats was November 1, 1979 at the Iceland Bowl & Ice Arena. At season's end, our record stood at 5 wins and 3 losses.

For anyone who thinks this was a slam dunk— starting a collegiate ice hockey team in the desert, I can tell you it wasn't. The Icecats were formed in my mind during the summer of 1977, so I was working on the whole process for two years before Paula and I actually made the move to Tucson. In fact, during that summer, I started taking a research class at the University of Arizona, working toward getting my master's degree in education.

When we got here permanently in 1979, a lot of people already knew who I was and what I was planning. The reception at the U of A has always been positive, from, back in those days, the president John Schaefer down through to athletic director Dave Strack.

Father Frank McCarthy at Salpointe Catholic High School was very supportive of me and my efforts with the Icecats. The only time I missed a day of teaching at Salpointe, and never once a day for illness, was when the Icecats had to take road trips. Teaching at Salpointe in 1979 and coaching the Icecats at the same time, made for a pretty hectic schedule. My department chairperson, Jim Flannery, also Salpointe's basketball and golf coach, was very supportive.

At one point, we even had discussions with the University about having hockey being named a varsity sport. That's why we played 33 exhibition games against NCAA Division I teams in the late 1980s. After we won the NCCHA national championship, we discussed it again, but it was not to be. The dream I had was to build a college hockey team in the desert at the U of A with American born hockey players. And that's what I did, notwithstanding the lack of varsity support from the University, because in the end, I accomplished what I set out to do.

I'm from Chicago and I can be a big time guy when necessary. I'm a friend of Don Rickles and Garth Brooks. I may be an absolute nobody; a blue collar guy, but this is my life. I grew up in Chicago with the Bears, the Black Hawks and the White Sox, and even what we refer to as the minor league team, the Cubs. When I was 14 years old, I took two buses and two ells (elevated railway trains) to Wrigley Field because I wanted to see major league baseball. I wanted to watch Hank Aaron and Roberto Clemente — players whom I've met and shook hands with when I was a kid. I didn't even think about coaching hockey.

I remember meeting Satchel Paige in Springfield, Illinois. At the time, the Springfield Redbirds were the Triple A farm team of the St. Louis Cardinals in Satchel Paige's home town and I ended up sitting in back of home plate during some games, more awestruck than anything. Years before, I saw Satchel come off the bus at Wrigley Field in Chicago — a big tall thin black man who everybody mobbed for his autograph. I was 16 or 17 at the time, but Satchel signed for me because I had his book, *I'll Probably Pitch Forever*, with me. He saw the book and signed it.

I remember going down to the Knickerbocker Hotel in the late 1960s, where the Pittsburgh Pirates were staying, and getting many Pirates' autographs and also getting a 'Best Wishes, Roberto Clemente' signature and actually shaking Clemente's hand.

On my back patio in Tucson, I have three chairs from the old Comiskey Park bolted into the concrete, along with the railing from the box seats. I also have a light from the light tower that I use for an end table. Whether it's my den or the sports room, there's Nellie Fox stuff all over the place.

I said before that baseball is my passion. My house is adorned with Nellie Fox material, including the room leading to my den where there's a big carpet-type towel, taking up the whole door, about Nellie Fox, giving to me by Mrs. Joanne Fox.

When I met Fox one on one, he was in an overcoat smoking a cigar about 18 inches, or so it seemed at the time. I went up to him and asked for his autograph and he declined. I can understand because he probably gets a lot of requests for his signature. I had enough nerve to go back to him and tell him that back in 1962 I had mailed both a birthday and Christmas card because I knew his birthday is on December 25. He smiled and signed an autograph for me. I was in the right place, at the right time, with the right information.

Some people wonder why I gravitated into hockey instead of baseball, but I don't think I ever gravitated away from baseball. I've coached 18 seasons of baseball. I played college baseball my freshman year. I've always played baseball, but I loved goaltending. I love hockey and skating, especially the kind of skating and playing that was done by my idol, Glenn Hall.

Early on, perhaps I thought anybody could be a baseball player because it's the American sport. But how many people could be skaters and hockey players? What it comes down to is that baseball is my passion and hockey is my job.

I coached baseball in Chicago and in Tucson — Babe Ruth league, Pony League, high school. I was most recently the varsity pitching coach for Sabino High School in Tucson. I love coaching. Baseball is a vehicle for me. For some of the kids I coach, they think I'm so cool because the personna I give them to latch onto is that I don't drink or smoke. I'm pretty conservative, I guess; they don't know that, but they think there's something about this guy that puzzles them. For some of these kids, I'm thought of as a mentor.

What you have to do is to try to get these guys to fulfill themselves. They have to learn to live and not simply exist in their quests. Maybe they don't know who they are. I want to know not only who they are, but what we can get out of them before they know what they are. We probably have a good idea of what we'd like them to be, but we have to give them a chance to figure it out for themselves.

People have asked me if I coach baseball with the same philosophy as I do hockey. The issue with hockey is that I get involved with kids over a four year period and spend a lot of time on the ice and in the locker room talking with them about how to succeed in the game. I also talk to them about the philosophy of life. I always try to get the kids to be aware of the importance of mom and dad in their lives, and also the commitment to academics. The philosophy doesn't change, but the M.O. does, whether it's baseball or hockey, in teaching life's lessons through these sports.

I don't think I'm cool. I think blue jeans and a black tee shirt are pretty much who I am. I never felt I was cool in the sense of the word because I was brought up much too conservatively. You couldn't be cool because you were to be the family priest, because you didn't swear and didn't do anything really bad because you were too God-fearing.

I don't think I ever really had a childhood because I was too busy being proper and pleasing other people — my parents and others. Now I can be more what I perceive as myself in wanting to attract their attention, whether at the hockey rink or in supporting the team. Sometimes, I want the players to take a chance on this coach so they can let down their guard and be real and actually open up to me about their lives outside sports.

I'm a great admirer of Abraham Lincoln and don't try to please people at all. However, I do try to be a good person, but I'm a renegade — a Thomas Jefferson-type of revolutionary, a pathfinder of sorts. We look at them as founding fathers and as great presidents. Well, Leo Golembiewski is the founder of the Arizona Icecats and has the philosophy of 'Why Not? Go for the whole enchilada.' Why shouldn't I be strict in order to achieve what I want on the ice and in the player's lives. I tell them — Don't do drugs, don't drink, be in control of yourself at all times.

Being cool sometimes embodies being square. It's impossible to admit that to those individuals who you are trying to teach. Very often I feel I'm a square peg in a round hole, and so much of my public persona is simply a facade.

Coach G doesn't smile — at least when people are looking at him. Occasionally, one can find the beginnings of a grin; perhaps only the slight turned up corners of his mouth. His public persona seems to forbid him from appearing more aloof, unaffected by the surroundings.

During a recent hockey game, the Icecats tied their opponents with essentially no time left on the clock. There's Coach G, stoically behind the bench, something he doesn't have to make an effort at because it comes naturally to him. He doesn't show any emotion at the players tying the game, instead of enjoying their happiness.

Coach G used to allow himself some smiles, like after making big saves in college, but says that smile left him quickly when he let the puck through the five hole in a big game. (In hockey parlance, the five hole is a goalie giving up a goal between his legs.) Glenn Hall told Leo, "You have to stay in focus — not too happy and not too sad."

I think I have a sense of humor, Coach G says, but it is very dry. Yet I think I have one of the best senses of humor you'll ever see. I'm genuinely a Don Rickles kind of guy because I'm good with the ad-lib and quick with my lip. My brother Chet has similar traits. I think either of us could liven up a wake.

I'm a funny guy, but when it comes through in coaching it has to have its place. Coaching and disciplining kids is not humor, it's my real job. But humor is a part of it, at times in the locker room. Some of the kids think I'm the funniest guy they ever met and it really blows the new kids away.

I want my players to jump as high as I require them, jump off the lip of the Grand Canyon if needed. That wouldn't be an impulsive jump because if they did it, it would come from the heart. That's where I want to reach them.

I don't think the players see me as one dimensional. Actually, how they really see me, I don't know, and I really don't care. As long as I get the grades out of them they should be achieving, then I can get the respect in their lives. It's important to me to want them to respect their lives. With the Icecats, we have this pyramid of family first, then academics and then hockey. The very star on the top is respect of your own life within your family. That's the top of the pyramid.

Academics have the ultimate place in playing hockey. The American College Hockey Association has a bylaw that you have to have a 2.0 grade point average in order to be eligible to play. I've had those rules in my organization from the beginning.

In the Icecat program, we graduate virtually 100 percent of our players. If you stay with us four years you'll graduate.

Sometimes you really don't realize you're an actual hockey player. I don't think I was a real hockey player in anybody's eyes when I was in high school until one Sunday afternoon when I took a stick across the mouth and got a tooth knocked out. I came to school on Monday morning looking like I had a catcher's mitt on my face and the kids finally said, 'I guess he is a hockey player.'

8.
Thoughts on a Coaching Life

There is such a thing as nurturing, even in coaching.

Before I came to Tucson to start a college hockey team for the University of Arizona with American-born players, I learned that minor league hockey had failed three times in Tucson during the 1970s. Later, they failed another two times. One of the biggest problems was there was no place to play and only a small practice rink.

After I formed the Icecats, for the first 9 years those players played every practice at the Iceland Arena on Speedway Boulevard. Back then, it seemed as if the only ice you could find in Tucson was in a glass — whether it be a mixed drink or a soda.

When you walked into the Iceland Arena, there was a 117 foot by 70 foot sheet of ice surrounded by cinder block walls on three sides, and sand on the fourth side. There was no glass around the ice. There were no locker rooms at the arena. The only thing we did have were benches, and of course, the ice itself.

Looking back at the beginnings of the Icecats, I guess you could say that we had some obstacles to overcome. At the time, hockey was dead in the water, nationally speaking, back then too.

Our goal early on with the Icecats was to attract people to see them play, and we were doing pretty well. We were drawing 5,000 to 6,000 people for every game. At the time, we were offering what we called $2 festival seating.

When I first started coaching the Icecats, we were getting a lot of positive comments about both the players and the coaching. I was being told all the time, "Coach, you make it look so easy." Of course, the reality is that it's not so easy — it's a lot of work, mentoring, heartache and determination.

Scotty Bowman, when he came to Tucson for NHL meetings at La Paloma Resort, pulled me aside after hearing what we — the players and I had accomplished over the years — and said to me, "What are you, a f***ing magician?"

I told him, "It's nuts. It's an impossible dream, but it's my impossible dream."

The people who criticized me when I first came on the scene in Tucson said I was too passionate. I was too rough with the players and others. They said I didn't deal with the media in the right way, always fighting for our kids and hockey.

My answer to them is this is the way I am, and this is the way I coach. It's worked pretty well, so I don't see the sense in changing how I go about it simply because someone wants to snipe at me from the other side of the boards. The Icecats have been a life's work for me. I've been doing this for 30-plus years. In fact, I defy anybody else to put up with the crap I have for 30 years and still accomplish what we have with these kids and with this team.

What's my secret of coaching? You might say I make it look so easy because I work 16 to 18 hours a day. Back in 1985 when we were the national champions of the NCCHA, it was the fifth full year of play for the Icecats and our sixth in existence. That first year, we only played a partial schedule of eight games, with no home games during our first two years. Home games were played at Oceanside in Tempe, Arizona.

For me, coaching has never has been about winning. It's been about getting the best out of the members of the team. It's the kids who are playing who count the most.

I've coached hockey for 39 years — 7 years of high school and 32 years of college. I've coached 18 seasons of baseball. Anybody in their right mind wouldn't have tried to do what I've done both in hockey and baseball coaching, but I still keep coming back, season after season. As I said, it's the kids who count. It's been a life's work.

Some people look at what we've accomplished with the Icecats ask, "How did you do it."

My response, depending on my mood, has occasionally been, "There's a fine line between love and hate, but also between brilliance and stupidity. Sometimes I don't know where those lines are."

Besides that philosophy, I also have a long suffering wife, Paula, who has loved me through it all, and stood behind me, and supported me all these years.

I really don't remember a time when I didn't want to be involved in hockey. Back in Illinois, when I was 12 years old, I even combed my hair like my idol, Glenn Hall. I would have thrown up before a game too, like he did, if I could have (but I didn't).

Wearing Jacques Plante's No. 30 at Rookie Camp with the St. Louis Blues at the Arena in 1972, (though I wore No. 1 throughout my career), I can still remember the scene like it was yesterday. I took two strides and then five steps and then went out onto the ice. I remember skating near the far goal before a game and wanted to stop a puck because I couldn't feel my legs. I could see thousands of fans wearing jerseys with Plante's No. 30.

While I didn't make the St. Louis Blues team, I still turned that love of hockey into something tangible, not only for me, but for hundreds and hundreds of kids who I've coached over the years. The way I coach with the Icecats is that I treat the kids in such a way that even if they never get an opportunity to play in the National Hockey League, I still want them to get that same feeling by playing for the University of Arizona Icecats.

When I look back over my hockey coaching career, I find that with nearly 1,000 victories in coaching hockey, it's been a blur.

But when I consider that accomplishment, I realize that I'm not in it to win games. What's important to me is that I teach kids about living and knowing who they are as soon as they can in life.

I want to improve their attitudes in life — toward their mom and dad, their siblings, friends and teammates. My philosophy with my players always has been that family always comes first. Then academics. And only then comes hockey.

9.
The Real Coach G

"I think people don't really know me because I throw up a defense mechanism. Perhaps it's partly from the film The Godfather, which I use to scare the pains in the ass away, but I've always had a modus operandi that my door is always open – just walk through the door. If you want to discuss something, come in and go ahead," says Coach G, "I'm here for you."

The real Coach G is someone pretty religious, contemplative, simple in one's desires to make him happy and a jack of all trades.

When Leo was a recommending scout for the Cincinnati Reds, his boss, Edwin Howsam, called him "a Renaissance man." To the kids, he's Coach G, but they also call him the G Unit, a nickname given to him by the kids at Sabino High School. "To get to the young people, you've got to be cool in their eyes," Coach says, but also points out they had a hard time saying "Golembiewski."

One of the images Coach G wants to convey to his players, and for that matter, to everyone else, is that he's excited to be involved in their lives.

"It's necessary for what I do," the coach says. "My detractors will say I'm cocky and arrogant, but I don't see it that way. I was put in a very difficult position in 1979 when I essentially had to invent college hockey here in Tucson. I had to nurture the idea, sell the game of hockey and sell the team called the Icecats, just like when I became the first hockey coach at Lyons Township High School in Illinois."

Coach G shrugs his shoulders. "Several years ago a friend, Bert Lee, wrote an article for CatTracks, a sports publication about University of Arizona athletics," coach says. "Bert pointed out that you have to come up with different words, different expressions and different modes of communication in order to catch people's eye. That's what I'm doing."

Coach shifts in his seat and stabs a forefinger in the air. "Look at Don Rickles, who's an absolute sweetheart no matter what he conveys through his stage presence. When Rickles's is on — he's on. When I was teaching at Salpointe Catholic High School, I was doing 55 minute classes, five times a day.

"Think of what Johnny Carson's entrance music was on the Tonight Show — Heeeeere's G," coach says. "Then you're on for 55 minutes for that class. You try to instill learning and project the importance of society to these kids, teaching American Government, Tucson history and Arizona history. Sometimes it seemed futile, because some seniors in high school didn't even know the names of the four mountain ranges around Tucson."

Coach G believes that if you're going to grasp your philosophy and take it as far as you can, then it can't be a philosophy that's only geared to your own personal perceptions or ways of communication.

"You have to be able to get up in front of people and tweak the message you want to give them," he says. "You have to talk to people in terms they understand, but at the same time, certainly not talk down to them. You have to talk to them in natural terms."

In the locker room before an Icecat hockey game, the common thread Coach G uses is preparation. He believes strongly players have to mentally prepare for what they are about to do. In Coach G's world, players must prepare themselves for practice, in order to work on the things they have to be able to do, whether it's skating, passing or shooting skills. He also believes that players can't work on any of those elements unless they are completely zoned in to the practice or game at hand.

Motivation, then, becomes one of the keys that Coach G uses to get the best, or at least, the most, out of his players.

"I try to motivate my players with as little use of the verbal as possible," Coach G. notes. "Pontification doesn't work with today's kids. Pressing the pedal to the metal is something you might get away with on a high school level, where you could treat the kids like you're the drill sergeant, like you're the boss."

"But that doesn't really fly these days because to be an effective leader you have to get into their very hearts, souls and minds," coach continues. "Not mind games, because they ultimately end up biting you in the butt because the kids will realize you are a phony. I get into their hearts and minds through their own personal self worth — the game itself and how they treat the game."

Coach G is a great student of history and uses that knowledge to motivate kids out on the ice.

"A couple of years ago, against Oklahoma, we lost both games by a single goal and still gave them the best games of the 15 they had played until then," he says. "Then we had a four game losing streak, and four of our overall six losses at that point in the season were by a single goal. So Saturday night after the Liberty game, which was our worst loss in 18 years, I knew what had happened."

The coach's eyes narrow. "I said to them, 'The zookeeper has taken over the zoo. When you come back here nine days from now', which was when our next game was going to be played, 'Your jobs are on the line. Your execution abilities are what's important. Whether I use two or two and a half lines because you guys can't cut it, makes no difference to me because we lost and we're not going to continue losing."

Part of the difficulty of coaching kids in the twenty-first century, the coach maintains, is their attitude toward life and their lack of responsibility and accountability.

"You have kids today who are so pompous, arrogant and rich they nearly have silver spoons in their mouths," Coach G says. "My biggest problem with the kids I coach in the Icecats organization during the last 10 years has been the kids think they have a right to play for the Icecats, instead of it being a privilege to play. There is no American Collegiate Hockey Association team that plays in a 7,000 seat arena like the Icecats do. In fact, there's not many NCAA Division I teams, that do either, so what we have is a big deal."

Handling players these days is much different than it used to be, Coach G maintains.

He doesn't like to use four letter words, but well . . . sometimes he does because, unfortunately, they are universal hockey vernacular words.

Coach G believes there are certain times when a coach has to use expressions to get to players because that's the only thing that is going to motivate the kid in the short term. We're talking about using vulgarities.

"I try to use the four letter F word as little as I can," Coach G says. "And that's pretty much a very universal hockey word that's part of the vernacular. But when I'm happy, I never use it. Yet sometimes when I feel like saying, 'Can I have your attention please?,' I may use it simply to bring the discussion down to their level of thought.

"It goes to my belief that losses are mine and the wins are theirs," he says. If a player gives me 100 percent at practice, in the locker room and in the game, then winning has nothing to do with anything. The important thing is how you perform and how you execute that will decide whether you win or lose. Part of my task is in getting players to not take advantage of their youth, money or lifestyle and concentrate on what's really important."

Coach G believes most students and players in college are pretty much self centered at that age.

"The way I approach the issue, when I talk to the players about general and specific things, I don't couch it in such a way that they have a chance to re-but what I'm saying," he points out. "I give them a chance to think about what I said because I don't want a response from them. And then, if I'm irritated enough to go to the philosophical plane, to attack the intangibles, then that is what I will do."

The game of hockey is simple at first glance, but impossibly difficult if one is not prepared by practice to perform properly. Shooting a puck, missing a pass, scoring a goal, making a save, giving up a goal through the 5 hole (between a goalie's legs), those are physical mistakes that Coach G can fix by more practice and motivation among his players.

Miss the rushing forward with your pass because you're not thinking, and it's a major problem.

One evening some years back, Coach and Paula hosted New York Yankee greats Bill "Moose" Skowron, Hank Bauer and World Series no-hit game pitcher Don Larsen at their house. After dinner they sat around the table and recalled the 1950s under their manager, Casey Stengel. They talked about physical mistakes that are going to happen, but also about mental errors, like missing the cutoff man with a throw from the outfield or throwing to the wrong base, which should not be tolerated. After the Yankees left at 2 am, they felt good about going to the ball park and playing for Casey again — the next day!

That's what mental preparation in Coach G's world is. It is discipline, dedication, sacrifice, responsibility, commitment, loyalty, honesty — all of those intangibles team players always take for granted. One of Coach G's maxims is that hockey is 75 percent mental and the balance, physical.

Participation in any sport — or any endeavor — is rooted in respect, the coach believes.

"The guys who cheat the game are the ones who are not preparing to be out there and not working hard at the discipline that it takes," Coach G says. "My coaching philosophy involves three levels — family, academics and hockey. A player's lifestyle and social life, whether its his girlfriends or drinking with his friends, cannot be in that triumvirate. If it is, it shows in the way the guy plays, in the way he doesn't execute, and in the malaise he has during practice or the laissez faire attitude he has on the ice."

Having a laissez-faire attitude in hockey is difficult to do because players are skating around the ice at speeds of up to 30 miles per hour and if the player doesn't pay attention to what he's doing, he could get hurt and you wouldn't be able to fulfill you're his own goals as an athlete. So skills are extremely important and their development are even more so.

Drills are the main-stay of any team practice, and hockey is no different from other sports in that respect. Flow drills, shooting drills, puck handling drills, skating drills, give and go drills, drills, drills, drills, drills, drills — each is as important at the next because a player never knows when he'll have to execute a particular drill during an actual game. Coach G once took the team captain and had him stand next to the coach and watch the drills from behind the bench so the captain would see what the coach sees and feel the frustration he feels at times.

With the Icecats, the team usually has three co-captains. It becomes a show of respect for the people who get those designations. Generally, the captains, and also the co-captains, will be on different lines when on the ice. Their basic job is to communicate with the referees, but they also are the lieutenants on the ice, the guys who marshal their team members into action. So essentially, Coach G has four or five guys who have his back on the ice. These are players who know what's going on and can help be part of the solution. That's what Scotty Bowman taught Coach G all those years ago.

Coach G emanates a stand-offish and don't-mess with me persona, yet he seldom yells at the players after a loss. Sometimes he'll yell after a win, but if the team loses, the game is over. That's when coach wants his players, and himself, to go home and think about the game, and hopefully, learn from it.

"Losing is a great teacher, but you can't afford to lose games to prove you're right," coach says. "Long ago I told my team, I don't want to have to prove to you boys that I'm right by us losing a hockey game."

Back when Coach G was coaching high school players at Lyons Township High School in Illinois, his teams went 302 wins, 43 losses and 20 ties during his seven years as coach.

"It's easy to win with 14 to 17 year olds players because they are more god-fearing, and I'm much more apt to scare the be Jesus out of them," Coach G says.

When he coached Babe Ruth league and Pony League baseball teams, the players thought that Coach G was the coolest guy in the world. But at age 16, Coach says, kids get a driver's license and discover that girls exist, to say nothing of worse things like getting into drinking alcohol or doing drugs. Then Coach G isn't quite as cool as they thought, but the Coach G philosophy doesn't change, so he simply has to work harder.

Glenn Hall taught Coach G not to take himself too seriously.

"Just stop the puck," he told me, coach says. "That's all you have to do. Glenn Hall was a flopper, which meant he wasn't afraid to drop to the ice, and

I was a flopper too, with good reflexes. As a goalie, if you're a flopper, it means you have quick reflexes to go down and then get back up, it means you're acrobatic."

So the coach uses his experience as a goalie with his players today. He remembers when he first faced a NHL player, Danny Grant.

"Grant was a 50-goal-scorer and a forward for the Minnesota North Stars," coach says. "When he took a slap shot on me, the puck was in and out of the net so fast that — badda bing badda boom — I didn't see it. But by the second day, I was starting to catch some of that stuff."

Coach G tells his goaltenders you can't get better unless your players shoot better in practice. He says that the shots that go upstairs, toward the top corners of the net, are the toughest. Goalies must always be seeking and finding the puck.

"I want my goalies to be able to make that high, quick glove save," Coach G says,. "but if the goalie never sees the shot, he doesn't have a chance. That's where we get to the heart of what the team is — hard work in the goal and on the ice — not because you make pasta for the team once a week or show NHL highlights from ESPN."

Coach G believes his players should play the game the way they practice, essentially playing to execute the drills, to get the job done. So when the Icecats have a two-on-one breakaway, Coach G expects them to convert that pass and then convert the shot. "The key," he says, "is in executing better than the other guy on the ice."

"I'm not a simple man, and yet I am," Coach G says, shrugging a shoulder as he says it. "I like nothing better than working with my hands on the cactus and other plants in the front and back yards on the acre Paula and I own in Tucson. I also like driving a 1972 Chevy Nova and a 1957 Chevy pickup.

"I like to go into my den where I have my 250 books on Abraham Lincoln, he continues with a look of excitement. In the den there's a picture of me and President Ronald Reagan on the wall, as well as endorsements signed by Abraham Lincoln and Mary Todd Lincoln. I also have a requisition order signed by George Washington — not really a great signature, but it's still something he actually held in his hand at the time."

One of coach's regrets in life is that by straying from the path to become a Benedictine monk, he would not be able to enter the priesthood.

"I'd love to be able to say Mass, more than anything else," Coach G says. "but not to forego my marriage to Paula."

Of his relationships with famous people and celebrities, Coach makes no apologies.

"I've talked to Don Rickles a lot in the last eight years or so, even if it's in Las Vegas before or after a show or here in Tucson or some other place he's performing," Coach G says. "It's very different seeing him orchestrate onstage and then seeing the kind of sweetheart he really is. I didn't realize the effect Don Rickles's persona had on me in college until I went back to my college reunion where everybody was using the word 'dummy.' That's classic Rickles and he gave me the persona to be funny, sarcastic, something much more than my boring personality. He was able to give me confidence in myself, which I never had before."

Ultimately, Coach G still doesn't have as much confidence in himself as he'd like to. He says he has as many faults, and sometimes more faults, than a lot of people, but looks to his Catholic faith as a source of inspiration.

"The first thing I did backstage when I met Don Rickles was kissed him on the cheek out of respect," Coach G says. "Later during the show, he gave me a thumbs up. Ever since then, we acknowledge each other with a kiss on the cheek as a sign of respect. It's both an Italian and Polish thing — you always kissed your uncles on the cheek. His manager, Tony Oppedisano, was impressed in that understanding of respect I had for Mr. Rickles."

Coach G credits Don Rickles with giving him the chutzpah to want to be a pro hockey player and not be only a divinity and seminary student.

Coach also has a strong friendship with Rex Allen Jr., who took Dan Fogelbird's song and made it 'Leader of the Band,' about his father.

"When I'm in a pensive mood, I'll take a song like that and put 10 CDs on my Durango seat and drive the 56 miles to the Holy Trinity Monastery by myself and go to the church to light some candles," coach says.

With Larry King, coach admits to always enjoying his radio show. He got to know Chris Castleberry, King's producer, and King pretty well through phone calls and then getting King to be guest of honor at the Icecats banquet in 1989, calling the banquet "one of the best we ever had."

Coach G met F. Lee Bailey through one of his player's fathers, Terry Wochok, a prominent Philadelphia lawyer who has served on the Arizona Icecats Board of Directors. Wochok arranged for F. Lee Bailey be the guest at the Icecats banquet in April 2006. As honorary captain, Bailey came out and skated with the team to center ice to open the season in 2006, and also did color commentary for the second and third periods. Bailey spent the first period on the bench with Coach G.

After Coach G's meeting with Johnny Cash and June Carter 15 years ago, he was reminded of Abraham Lincoln. Coach felt Johnny Cash had the same dark hair, intense black eyes, and carried himself the same way that Lincoln did.

Garth Brooks is yet another singer-celebrity acquaintance of Coach G, as well as the late Senator Ted Kennedy, among many other entertainers, politicians and sports figures.

10.
Who Coach G Really Is

Coach G has a goalie's physique with dark, bushy, arched eyebrows; straight graying hair with streaks of brown in it; and droopy eyelids over dark brown eyes. As a player, he had a dark brown mop of hair topping off his 5-foot 11-inch, 190-pound frame. He's still got a reserved kind of look, but don't let that lull you into a false sense that he's easy prey because he's not. He's humble, often self-depreciating, yet always frank and outspoken.

He says three rosaries each day, probably harking back to his Benedictine training. He likes to say, "I'm a monk in blue jeans and a tee shirt," but if you believed that you'd be selling the man short.

"The classroom is my office," Coach G says, offering the observation that the classroom could just as well be a sheet of hockey ice or a locker room, as well as a traditional classroom. "I try to teach kids it's important that you learn from history. You have to learn from the past in order to have a better future."

Coach G gets reflective and sips his Diet Pepsi. "When you see all the great books out there and the many significant things that are happening in the world, sometimes it hard to even fathom doing something like I'm doing and believing people would even be mildly interested in it. But they are."

The coach isn't wrong in his assessment. The feeling people have about Leo Golembiewski is that you either love him or hate him. There doesn't seem to be much middle ground when it comes to the coach — either what you get from him or what he expects from you.

"You can't think it's sort of okay because I shoot from the hip, and I don't pull any punches," Coach G says, stone-faced. "You definitely will know where I stand, whether it's politics, hockey or the Chicago White Sox." He pauses for a moment, but his gaze continues to hold you. "I'm very frank and direct. I don't mask displeasure well, but I do mask happiness well."

Any displeasure that the coach feels doesn't show up in his coaching.

"I've always believed that as a coach, it's my responsibility to win hockey games," he says. "We win a hockey game if the players win. When we lose hockey games, they're my losses. Nobody beats up Leo Golembiewski more than Leo Golembiewski." There's the smallest hint of a turned up corner on Coach G's mouth, the closest he gets to a smile.

"When we lose a game I find myself being more pensive and I will show displeasure in between periods with the hope of motivating the players in the locker room," Coach G continues. "But when the game is done, there ain't nothing to talk about, whether it's any mistakes that I made on the bench, (which I do), or the mental and physical mistakes the players make on the ice."

Coach G does his philosophical pontificating after a loss to try to instill in his players the idea that it's not winning or losing that really matters, it's what you bring to the table, or in this case, the ice, with your heart and soul. That essentially leads to coach's overall philosophy — family comes first, academics are second, and hockey is third.

One of the ways that Coach G approaches dealing with his young charges is to make himself vulnerable.

"I make myself vulnerable to my players only because I think if you really believe in what you do, then the harder your profession is for people to deal with," he says. "Dealing with the players either one-on-one or as a group, is very hard to do. I want to get something out of them, but they might not know they even have it in themselves. This is especially true of American-born hockey players as opposed to the Canadian-born. The junior players who come to me now are from 14 different states."

The way Coach G coaches in Arizona is that if you've never played in the National Hockey League, take a deep breath because the Icecats are the closest you're going to get.

"There are more Eastern Europeans now in the NHL than there are Americans," he observes, shaking his head. "In Arizona we make up player hockey cards, produce posters of them to distribute, and get them to sign autographs for thousands of fans. They have this whole cult existence, something the mainstream sports of basketball and football will never have because hockey is a cult sport. And the Icecats are a cult team with our own fans."

Back to that love or hate relationship that many people have with Coach G.

"People in the hockey world who aren't a part of the Arizona Icecats don't like me because they want to be part of it," coach says. "And they can't be part of it because we are our own brand of craziness. And I'm the one that everybody loves to love, and everybody loves to hate."

But Tucsonans love the Icecat hockey team.

"There's nowhere we can't go that people don't go crazy over us," Coach G says. "But there are other hockey people who said it couldn't be done, that we'd never succeed with a team made up of American-born hockey players. They didn't give us support because they didn't think it could be done. Once it was done and continued to grow, they figure there must be some other reason of why that happened, why it became a success, but not because of Leo Golembiewski."

So has success spoiled Coach G or does he still strike fear into his players?

"Oh yeah, I do," he says. "I'm the authoritarian figure. Do the kids respect the day that I got 600 wins, a national championship and 8 appearances in the Final Four?" Coach G shrugs his shoulders and his eyes reveal nothing. "I don't think they really think about it. But what they're interested in is NOW, in hockey NOW. Or maybe the NHL game last night or the one that's going to be on tonight."

Coach G's hockey players are seemingly not interested in where he came from or how he got to be where he is in life. The coach believes that because he's an educator with a bachelor's degree in history and a master's degree in education, he believes people learn from history — that it's extremely important to learn from the past in order to have a better future, but the kids of today, he observes, don't want to hear about that.

Dealing with college aged kids can be a tricky business. And often, dealing with their parents can be even trickier.

"With the high school kids, what some of the parents didn't like, ultimately, was I could tell their kids we had a 10 pm curfew and they couldn't allow their kids to come home at one o'clock in the morning," Coach G says. "I tell these players they should be anti — anti-drug, anti-drinking and anti-chicks. I suggest they don't go out with only one girl, go out with twelve. Don't get too tangled up in life. A singular relationship could cause them to lose focus on their personal goals."

It's Coach G's firm belief the sooner a man knows who he is, the sooner that man will know what he wants. Kids from 13 to 15 years old know what they want, he says, and "the thing that has kept more American, Canadian and European hockey players from reaching their sports goals have been the triumvirate of drugs, drinking and girls."

In working with his college hockey players, Coach G tries to instill in each of them a sense of self worth — that they are individuals, yet still have to interact with other players and have to deal with team concepts.

"I try to get at them personally," Coach G says. "I want them to be cool, to stay away from drugs and not drink. These kids should play the game at college as if they were a pee wee hockey player, like a 10 or 12 year old. It means they're still having fun, staying open-minded to the ever-changing game and themselves."

The players who buy into that concept are happier kids on the team, Coach G maintains. The pressure of winning with the Arizona Icecats can be nearly unbearable because the Icecats can't draw fans unless they win. Coach G says that shouldn't be the pressure on the players, only on him.

"I want my players to play the style we preach in practice," he says. "I want you to execute the plays the way we want you to play. Our style is pretty simple; it's up and down the ice."

There has to be accountability too if you're playing for Coach G. You have to work hard to achieve at anything you do.

"Some kids don't like their mom or dad, for whatever reason," coach says. "So a sport like hockey becomes a vehicle for me to teach the players about life. But it's still only a game; hockey ain't war; Iraq is war."

Coach G tries to give his players a little bit of perspective.

"The four years of undergraduate college can be the best years of your life.," coach maintains. "But if you're an athlete, you have to make sure you temper your attitude toward the social, the academic and the athletic. You've got a lot of things going on and you've got to do justice to the most important things, which is why family and sibling relationships are number one, academics are number two; and hockey is number three. So social is down on the list."

Coach G notes that NHL Hall of Famer goalie, Stanley Cup winner and one of the top 10 goalkeepers of all time —Glenn Hall — as well as coach Jimmy Roberts, and coach Scotty Bowman, were part of an array of charismatic, over-achieving, stellar hockey players and coaches who had a chance to shape the game and also shape the mind and philosophy of a kid from Lyons, Illinois.

"I know so many of these people, and to be able to see what they've done with their lives and what they've accomplished, I think either 'I've done that' or 'I'd like to do that'" Coach G says. "But for kids today, everything's on a video screen or its a sound byte or a highlight on television or the internet. The players aren't real for them, so there's nothing in depth."

The key, the coach says, is a belief you have in yourself, as well as a respect you should have for the game.

"It's all encompassing," he says. "You want to dress like a pro, act like a pro. When I was 12 years old I combed my hair like Glenn Hall and copied the way he played. You believe in the dream."

But the coach's early dream of playing pro hockey was an impossibility at the time, or so it seemed.

"Growing up in the early 1960s and going to college from 1967 to 1971 at St. Procopius, (now Benedictine University), I didn't think it was possible," Coach G says. "Then I got the opportunity to practice with the St. Louis Blues, took shots from them, and they picked on me and loved me. But it still was an impossible dream."

After graduating from college in 1971, Coach G was chosen to attend the Blues' Pro Camp. At the camp there were nine goalies, including six NHL goalies, a draft pick, a kid from the University of Toronto and me.

"Back at that time, you simply didn't get an opportunity to do that unless you had something special, something that attracted their attention," coach says. "At the camp, we each had a huge chance to be somewhere and do something special, and that seemed like an impossible accomplishment."

The American College Hockey Association (ACHA) doesn't allow its hockey teams to offer scholarships (even though it caters to the American players). Yet the top six or eight players on the Icecats could play at the level of the National Collegiate Athletic Association (NCAA), the coach maintains.

"What we tried to do in Tucson right away in 1979 was to build a serious college hockey program with American-born hockey players," he says. "We came at a time when all that was available was the Tucson Convention Center, an operation that got burnt three times by the minor leagues in the seventies, including 1978 and then 1979, the year before I got there."

After he put together the Icecats, inventing the name "Icecats" in 1980, the team played in eight games its first year. Home games were played at Oceanside Arena in Tempe, Arizona. The second year, the Icecats joined the Rocky Mountain Hockey Association and played all of their home games in Tempe. It wasn't until the spring of 1981 that the Icecats played two games in Tucson, just as a lark, the coach says, against California State Northridge.

Fan response to those early games was overwhelmingly positive.

"They went nuts — they were crazy," Coach G says. "Of course people said in the early years the only reason we drew fans was there was beer available at the rink. Then they said, 'Don't worry, it's a fad. It won't catch on.'" And then all of a sudden, the Arizona Icecats were still drawing fans and they were still packing the house. Well, that's because they sell beer, according to what the naysayers spout. But for all these years?

The early days were difficult, to say the least. The Icecats had no full size sheet of ice to hold practices on — they used the 70 by 117 foot Iceland rink on East Speedway Blvd. A standard size hockey rink is 85 by 200 feet. Every drill coach used was designed to make that smaller rink seem larger.

"I remember walking into Iceland in August of 1979, and I told the Tucson Hockey Club people, 'I'm Leo Golembiewski and I'm here to start an ice hockey team with the University of Arizona," Coach G says. "They laughed me out of the building."

Those same people, two or three years later, unsuccessfully tried to take the Icecats team away from Coach G, even though the team was supposedly doomed from the start not to succeed. But succeed it did, and with Coach G at the helm.

The team name — the Icecats — had an interesting beginning. What made Coach G think of Icecats was it was a parody on Wildcats, the University of Arizona mascot and team name.

"We didn't want to be known as the Wildcat Icers, which is what we were known as for our first two years or so," coach says. "I almost made us the Snowcats, but ultimately went with Icecats, which now has been borrowed by other college teams and a minor league professional team.

"Scotty Bowman, Glenn Hall, Bobby Hull, Al Arbour, Sid Abel, all those guys influenced me in some fashion." Coach G points out. "When I saw Al Arbour at the Chicago Blackhawks reunion in 1996, he remembered me and gave me a big hug. He always was a hard-working player and a great coach — all class."

The Icecats were an enigma from day one, and we still are, according to Coach G.. And perhaps Leo Golembiewski is an enigma as well.

"The real Coach G is someone who people don't know," he says. "The only ones who come close to knowing who I am are the players who I befriended and helped through their everyday lives. These are the people who know my weaknesses and my strengths, what I like and what I don't like."

Coach G also has been involved with the Ara Parseghian Medical Research Foundation, which has as its goal finding a cure for Niemann-Pick Type C disease, a genetic disorder that primarily strikes children.

"When Michael Parseghian was dying, he loved Garth Brooks, but they couldn't get to Garth," coach says. "Cindy Parseghian found out I knew Garth and they approached me about Michael wanting to meet him. Me being the flamboyant guy that I can be, I called them back and said, 'Don't worry about it. Garth's coming in June and I'll take care of it.'"

By that time, Garth Brooks already was a legend in the music business, but Coach G truly did have an inside track to Garth Brooks.

"I called and said to Garth, you have to do me a favor," coach said. "This kid is dying and he loves you, I need six tickets and I want you to meet him in person." Coach G turns on the hint of a smile again. "He says, 'Sure coach, no problem.'"

At the concert in McKale Center at the University of Arizona, Michael Parseghian, his parents and siblings had front row seats. Garth Brooks met with all the kids, as well as Mike and Cindy Parseghian.

One of Coach G's proudest accomplishments, in these days of college basketball and football players jumping to the professional leagues after a year or two in school, is that his graduation rate of hockey players is 100 percent. Everybody who stays with the team for four years, graduates, the coach says.

And turnover on the team? Usually once someone makes the team, because Coach G is a softie at heart, but also because he's a mentor more than a coach, it means that player will never get cut, though Coach G and his assistant coaches all made the final decisions on the final roster.

"We're the mentor in these kids' lives; hockey is the vehicle," Coach G says. "Hockey is only the sidebar to their lives."

It's important to coach to be a mentor because he's first an educator. He originally wanted to be a Benedictine monk because they taught and coached. He says he never wanted to be a parish priest, not when he saw the difference he could make as a teacher and coach.

Does Coach G have any regrets at not becoming a Benedictine monk?

"The way I couch it is this — I'm an oblate of St. Benedict's right now, at Holy Trinity Monastery in St. David, Arizona," he says. "So as much as I pale in my life of being a good monk, the only thing I actually regret that I could have done in my life was to change bread and wine into the Body and Blood of Christ."

Coach G considers himself a monk in blue jeans and a tee shirt. He doesn't sell his religion and doesn't wear it on his sleeve, but he does live the philosophy. He calls himself religious in an unreligious way, saying three rosaries every day.

"Their quality maybe isn't that good, but it's my faith that sustains me, from a physical and psychological sense," he says.

And then there's Paula. Her presence has loomed large in his life. They have been married more than 30 years and she's the most supportive person in Coach G's close-knit family.

"I don't know if I'm a good person or not, but I don't think I'm a bad person," coach says. "I try not to judge people, but I have tried to live my life in an honest attempt to be fair and true to people."

11.
The Road to a Hockey Career

At every practice, I'm on the ice. Being on the ice makes you a part of the practice, a part of the team, a part of the game. You can yell from the bench and talk to the players from the bench, but it's not as effective as when I'm able to skate over to a player and instruct him.

At the time that I hurt my achilles tendon, I went through a two year period where I didn't skate at all. I wasn't on the ice with the players during any of the team practices. I think the fact I wasn't on the ice with them definitely hurt in their instruction during those two years.

I grew up playing hockey on a river before moving onto indoor ice. I think it's important I'm out there with my players, mixing it up with them at center ice, getting tight with them in the corners, passing the puck to them and shooting the puck at our goalie. I'm pretty sure there are not a lot of 60-plus-year-old ex-hockey players who skate every day during the winter.

I skate because I enjoy skating. I don't think there's anything I like doing more as a hockey player than skating because when I wasn't goaltending, I was skating outside or whenever else I got the chance.

In terms of a hockey team, a goalie should be your best skater. You've got to be up and down, going down to your knees or even flat to block a shot. You have to be able to move laterally, back and forth in the crease. A goalie has to be cat-like, in terms of the kind of reflexes he should have. That's one of the main things Glenn Hall taught me as a teenager — the goaltender should be the best skater on the team. When I couldn't skate and could hardly walk for two years because of the achilles tendon problem, it touched my soul deeply because I took so much pride in skating.

Could I skate like the wind now like I used to be able? I can honestly say if I didn't have a lack of confidence and lack of strength in my achilles tendon, I could still get up to a pretty good speed. I can also tell you I don't want to look like an old man out there. I can still shoot and skate. Age is age, that's a given, so you really can't fool yourself, but I was very proud of my skating ability and what I did as a player.

When I look at all the physical problems I've had during my skating and coaching careers — the congestive heart failure, the type 2 diabetes, the various serious infections, I thank God I'm still alive, let alone still doing things like skating, shooting and mixing it up with the players on the ice.

Losing weight has been a huge achievement for me, because I certainly look different, but I also feel a little bit better. I went from 283 to 220 pounds. It took me a little more than three years to shed those pounds, but the result has been remarkable. I do feel much better. I move better. I hope it will put some years on my lifespan.

I've always lacked self confidence and a positive sense of self image. Losing all that weight actually gave me a new self image and more self confidence.

Can I put my finger on why I think I lack of self confidence? Sure, I can do that. I was born and raised as a conservative, Polish Catholic, and when I was growing up I was taught to be reserved and more earthbound from a psychological standpoint. I was afraid to be like everybody else because I had to be more proper at all times than everyone else. I had to keep my nose to the grindstone and keep on working and keep up with expectations. These values were instilled in me by the twin educators of my family and my religion.

The reason I love the Benedictines, and why I'm an oblate of St. Benedict, is they did so much in reforming me educationally. A bunch of my friends and I skated with Father Richard Shonka when he was in his early 70s. Besides skating, we also lifted weights with Father Fidelis and we played tennis with former Abbot Dismas Kalcic, who then was Father Dismas, an economics professor.

I started the Benedictine thing as a freshman in high school. I was a divinity day student at St. Procopius Academy, which is now Benet Academy in Lisle, Illinois, and commuted every day because we didn't live in that town. This was an all boys Catholic high school that became a coeducational institution the year after I graduated in 1967.

At the time, if you were a divinity student, you took the classes that prepared you for the priesthood, and if you were a regular student you took the standard academic classes without the divinity component.

When I was a freshman at St. Procopius, I absolutely knew I wanted to be a Benedictine monk. I was convinced that was the way for me. So I always say I spent 6 years studying to be a Benedictine; the four years of high school

70

and the first two years at St. Procopius College/Illinois Benedictine College/ Benedictine University.

Brother Joseph, who is now in his 90s, said to me in 1977 when I married Paula, "I guess you're not coming back." The monks still had held out hope until then I might change my mind and stay with the Benedictines. I think a lot of the Benedictines thought I would because I had been so dedicated. Future Abbot Hugh Anderson at St. Procopius Abbey, at the time seemed convinced I would stay. While I did leave, that entire eight years I spent under the influence of the Benedictines are the main years that determined who I was to become.

I never thought I'd moved away from being a Benedictine because I wanted to continue my college hockey, so I finished my college career and then was one of nine goalies at Pro Camp with the St. Louis Blues in Flint, Michigan in 1971.

I didn't play a lot of organized hockey until I got to college because it wasn't a sport I could afford to play. There weren't many rinks in our area, so there wasn't a lot of ice time for people like me, let alone anyone else. To do what I did as a player, whether you knew people or impressed people or not, to go where I did in hockey, playing virtually no organized hockey until college was unusual. Essentially, I was a self taught goalie who was fortunate to fall under the tutelage of Glenn Hall. I tried to emulate him in every way.

The whole hockey thing for me is that it was so self initiated, self orchestrated, self driven, it was the only way for me to do it. There was really no way this should have happened to a blue collar kid from Lyons, Illinois, which is truly a blue collar town. My parents were representative of a lot of people in Lyons. My dad, Chester, was a truck driver. My mom, Irene, worked in the National Tea Food Store and before that in a factory during the time my brother Chet and I were growing up.

The annual Leo Golembiewski Golf Tournament has been successful over the years, raising money for the Muscular Dystrophy Association, the DARE program and the Icecats. Getting to know all the people I've met through the games of hockey and baseball, well it seems it was almost impossible. I know I put on a personna of self confidence and arrogance, which is why I'm hard to understand, but in total humility, the people who know me, love me and understand me, see the outside person as the façade. Other people have no idea what the real Leo Golembiewski is like.

I've always been very protective of myself. I'm sometimes perceived as arrogant, but I never looked at myself in that way. I'm the first to admit I'm not outgoing. It's difficult for me to be personable. In my mind, I think no one would be interested in me. I ask myself, "Why would anyone be interested in Leo Golembiewski?" It keeps people away a little, but the door is open always — walk through it.

When I look at the things that really interest me, I see the highlights of every year I'm alive. I treasure my relationship with Paula and our 30-plus years of marriage, the downtime I spend at the Holy Trinity Monastery planting trees, or simply listening to Johnny Cash, Garth Brooks or classic rock on CDs in the car while going from place to place.

After one of my golf tournaments, I met All American Rejects, a group of kids in their 20s who play good music. These are the kind of guys who appeal to teenagers. They were all very gracious with their time and I gave them all Icecat tee shirts, which all were too big for them. When I saw them in concert, I was leaning against a pole and it struck me that I enjoyed their music because its pop rock. The music was great and coming home, I told Paula it was great to see how much they liked performing together.

I've known a lot of celebrities, but a guy like Don Rickles doesn't appeal to me only because of his humor. When I was a 12 year old, I listened to his "Hello Dummy" album and knew right away he was like me, or more important, I was like him. I wasn't a joke teller, but could respond to friends similarly to his type of humor.

I'm the coach. I'm Leo, and I've never really liked the name Leo. I was named after my dad's brother who died in his 20s.

Many types of people — folks like Glenn Hall — were a great influence in my life because you don't get there without some sort of guidance. For instance, I met Casey Kasem and Jerry Lewis several times, and each of them taught me to reach for the stars but keep my feet on the ground.

I loved Nellie Fox, the second baseman for the Chicago White Sox who was inducted into the Baseball Hall of Fame in 1997, because he was the little guy who was always fighting harder than anyone else. I got to know Mrs. Joanne Fox and keep in contact with her. I drove from Tucson to Cooperstown, N.Y., with some friends to be there for his induction into the Baseball Hall of Fame.

When I got involved in college hockey at St. Procopius College, they knew I was coming from across the street at the Academy. That's right; the high school was literally across the road from the college. The college's goalie had just graduated when I arrived, and I worked so hard I started every game for four years. I'm proud to say that each of the four years I led the league in saves. This was the old Midwest Collegiate Hockey League, headquartered out of Joliet, Illinois. Our team was terrible, but that is how you lead the league in saves every year. During my senior year, we went 13 wins and 6 losses.

During my college career, I only had two shutouts, but for those two shutouts, it was like I stood on my head and really played well. I played with a hurt knee in the semi and finals against Northern Illinois. During the game where we shut them out 6 to 0, a game for which I received wide acclaim, the guys in front of me played really well. I made a lot of saves, but the guys out front did a spectacular job and we shut out an undefeated team. At the time, I was fortunate enough to get the glory in the Chicago Tribune's sports pages.

The next night we played Lewis University for the championship (this was in 1971). The guys and I played well in that game and we beat them by a score of 5 to 3. I must have made more than 30 saves.

I'm a difficult person to get to know. I tend to be much more philosophical; I go after kids' psyche. The key to my coaching over the years is motivation. If you cheat the game you'll never like me. I know immediately if a player is a scammer. I consider the game something sacred. It's not something that should be taken lightly. A player should never think he's bigger than the game.

I'm a student of the game, but I'm not an X's and O's coach. How can you be working with X's and O's? Players skate around the ice at 30 mph. If the puck's traveling at 100 miles an hour, where are you supposed to be if you've done the right thing?. Where are the other five guys on the other team — your four teammates? It's almost like zone hockey, but you really have to play the game by areas of responsibility. If someone doesn't do his job, the other team scores.

So much of hockey is common sense. By the same token, so much of life is common sense. But important that you know your weaknesses. I know mine and I'm not happy with them, but that's okay because I compensate in other ways. Hockey, and even baseball, are vehicles where you can get at the heart, mind and soul of a young person to make him better and help him get to know himself so he can be a better and stronger person in the real world.

The sooner you get to know who the hell you are the better. I'm a firm believer in that. I like to cite the quote from the 'Godfather' — "Women and children can afford to be reckless; not men." I take that quote, and whenever it applies, use it to get across my point.

Sometimes a hockey team will have a few players on it I can't stand, and vice versa, because they're scammers, but it's important not to let them temper you. The bottom line is you have to do what's best for the team. Whether you liked a player or not didn't matter; if he was good enough, he made the team.

I became a teacher and high school coach after attending my rookie camp Sid Abel invited me to in 1972. When I came home from the camp, I still had a chance to go to the minor leagues. Sid told me I had the potential to play in the National Hockey League, but he didn't have the power to get me there.

So, I turned it all over for education. I became a substitute teacher at Lyons Township High School in LaGrange, Illinois. You couldn't get into the school on a permanent basis because of tenure. All those teachers at LaGrange had been around since Abraham Lincoln was in the White House, or so it seemed. I wound up being the coach of the hockey club. I also wanted to get as much classroom experience as possible, so I became the super substitute for a few years, subbing for everything, from physical education to biology.

At the time, I took the 13 to 17-year old hockey players and applied my hockey knowledge to them, trying to teach them the basics, and later the advanced elements of the game. The kids are an exceptionally captive audience at that age. They thought I was very cool, but I always was pro parents. Part of my job as a teacher and coach was to make the parents of these kids look good.

Before long, I found myself branching off into running an ice hockey rink in Chicago, which I did for seven years. It seems like I couldn't stay busy enough during those years. Now, I wish I had the extra time.

My dad died in 1976 in Tucson. My mom wanted to go back to visit Chicago and while I was here in Tucson, I took my first class in my master's degree — a research class — at the University of Arizona. I knew I couldn't stay at high school level in terms of coaching because there was nowhere for these kids to go in hockey. So I came to Arizona and started planting the seeds of ice hockey here two years before I founded the Icecats team.

In February of 1979, I saw Scotty Bowman at the old Chicago Stadium the night he won his 300th game and told him I could go to the college level and start a hockey team at the University of Arizona. He told me, "Go do it and keep in touch with that dream."

At Easter break, when Paula and I came to Tucson to visit my mom, I went to Salpointe Catholic High School and met with principal Father Frank McCarthy, O.CARM. I told him I needed a job and was coming to Tucson to start an ice hockey team at the University of Arizona. He thought I was crazy, but because of my Midwest education at Benedictine University, he hired me to teach religion.

When I started teaching there in August, my salary was $8,700 for the 1979-1980 school year. I was teaching American Government to seniors and coaching baseball. During that trip, meeting University of Arizona president John Schaffer and athletic director Dave Strack were major accomplishments too.

12.
Coaching, Teaching and Life Thoughts

Building a hockey team with American born players at the University of Arizona got its start during the seven year period when I was coaching at the high school level in Illinois. I had some pretty good hockey players on my teams, and I believe there were players who should certainly have been afforded a chance to play NCAA Division I hockey. At that time, they were kind of passed over because it was mostly the Canadian players who got the scholarships. It was frustrating for me to see good players being passed over and not get a lucky break, even though they deserved it.

I visited Tucson for the first time in 1972 when I drove my mom and dad out from Illinois. My mom and dad had been in Tucson in the late 1960s, but by 1972 my dad's health was getting worse, so that's why I decided to drive them out. When we got out here we stayed in my cousin's house on the east side. I hadn't intended it, but I fell in love with the desert and mountains, and in the back of my mind I thought this would be a great place to live some day.

I was scheduled to go back to Illinois for the second year at the St. Louis Blues rookie camp, so I wasn't thinking of moving to Arizona at that point. I still had hopes and dreams of being a pro hockey player. I was not thinking about coaching hockey, even though I'd been coaching baseball since I was 18 years old. So after that second "cup of coffee" with the Blues, I got the coaching and teaching job in Illinois.

I coached both varsity and junior varsity hockey for the first couple years, then varsity only for the next five years. I coached, besides working at the ice rink and doing substitute teaching. So I've always been a workaholic and to this day that absolutely has not changed.

I came back out to Tucson and visited in 1973, 1974 and 1975 because mom and dad had moved here permanently in 1973 and bought a place at 22nd Street and Craycroft Road. I brought Paula out to Tucson in the summer of 1975, in August. What a time to introduce your bride-to-be to the desert. We were planning to be married in October of 1977.

My dad died in 1976 and my mom was then living on her own in Tucson. I couldn't do anything about that because of my hockey career and work in Chicago, but in 1977 I came out to Tucson for a month and I started my first class toward my master's degree. I had never even been on the University of Arizona campus until then. For me, being born and raised in the Chicago area, it was the Bulls, the Black Hawks and the White Sox. I had no affinity to any college other than Benedictine University and that was NAIA at the time and now NCAA Division 3.

When I got on the University of Arizona campus, I met Dr. Paul Allen, who became my advisor for my first research class. I figured if I wanted to be a college coach I should have a master's degree. Doctors Don Clark and Glenn Pate also figured prominently into my MEd. degree.

It was 1977 when I took a long look at hockey in Tucson and still decided to start the Icecats here, even though minor league hockey in town had failed a few times. My formal move to Tucson was in August of 1979, and Paula came out in October. I returned to Chicago that month to see Pope John Paul II and was fortunate enough to be one of 5,000 who saw him at Five Holy Martyrs Parish on the south side. Then we returned together to Tucson.

I didn't approach the Iceland Bowl and Ice Rink on East Speedway until I moved permanently to Tucson. It was a 20 lane bowling alley in the front and a half size ice rink in the back. It was there I tried to make a couple extra bucks, doing a full time job for part-time pay.

In 1985 I secured a full time position at Iceland which paid more than I made at Salpointe, which meant leaving the school because I couldn't continue to do both jobs. Besides, coaching and running the Icecats had gotten too big. I couldn't get everything done.

I miss teaching very much, but I certainly enjoy teaching hockey. However, you really can't instruct someone in shooting and skating — you have to accomplish those instructions through drills. Then, when you see an opening, you make adjustments here and there by calling a kid over to the bench or to the boards and talking to him about the adjustment you'd like him to make.

My philosophy of coaching is founded in the intangibles needed to be successful. There are seven of them — discipline, dedication, sacrifice, commitment, responsibility, honesty and loyalty.

I became a hockey coach to give back to the American player what I learned from the strongest coaches in the history of the game —Scotty Bowman, Al Arbour, Emile Francis and Jimmy Roberts. All those people influenced me.

In my years of coaching, my philosophy has never changed. However, the modus operandi I've used with the players has changed over the years because the players are different.

For instance, there's a big difference between coaching high school and college players. You have to sell yourself a great deal more on the college level. On the high school level the kids are e a captive audience. They go to the high school and you're their high school coach. So your philosophy and technique is what they are because they belong to the school.

At the college level, on the Icecats team, I have kids from 16 different states who are between 18 and 24 years old. These kids know more than me, or so they think — just like when you were 18 and you knew everything too. So I have to sell myself, and I put up with all sorts of things because of the age group these kids represent.

Back on the high school level, I didn't mentor as much. I didn't have to. It was 'I'm the coach and this is what I say and it's my way or the high way.' I used that approach in a good sense, in order to instill the discipline needed in the players and the style of play I wanted them to use.

The Icecats have the same style of play and same philosophy from my early teams to the current one. But I have to adjust the way I coach because of the temperament of the players. In the past ten years the players have changed in how they look at playing for the Icecats and now consider it as their right, not as a privilege.

In the locker room before a game, the players will be talking about the fans and friends they have coming to the game. I'm sure it's the same in NCAA Division 1 teams to a point because they play in front of big venues like we do, but the guy who coaches Division 1 has the cat by the tail because he has those scholarships hanging over them, and we have nothing.

We charged a $1,000 commitment fee to play on the Icecats. Arizona State University charges $2,800 per player. You don't even get on the ice without paying that fee. At DePaul University, the fee was $3,500. Most teams charge between $2,500 and $3,500 to play for teams in ice rinks that draw 50 fans. The Icecats are playing in an arena that seats 7,000 and we're drawing 4,000 fans to games. They're exciting games and the fans are a big part of that. The cost to play there is much more expensive for a weekend than many people realize and after all the expenses are paid most of the settlements aren't great. The Icecats didn't get any of the parking receipts and very little of the concession dollars.

The Icecats practiced for their first nine years at Iceland Bowl and Ice Rink on a half size ice sheet. For the first two years, we played our home games in Tempe, 120 miles away. After that, we played home games at the Tucson

Convention Center.

During our first seven years on the convention center ice, we practiced on Friday mornings, doing a light skate because the ice would be put in just for those two games on Friday and Saturday nights. It wasn't until 1988 when Iceland closed that I talked to new Convention Center Director Bill Joe Varney, a friend and 30-year employee of the University of Arizona into putting ice in permanently for the Icecats. Of course there were fewer events going on back then and the convention center tried to accommodate us more. From 1988 to 1995 the only ice we had was the TCC ice. If it was available to skate on and practice, then we did; if it wasn't, we didn't.

In 1995 the new rink on the East side opened and we skated there until 2007. Sometimes we had great afternoon times and sometimes we had to skate late at night. Now we practice two hours in the evenings if the ice is available. Since 2007, like prior to 1995, there were very little consistent practices. The coaching staff and players did the best we could with little practice.

Hockey can be a very challenging game. Getting the puck up off the stick and past the goalie is one of the hardest things for players to master. It's difficult because you have to have a lot of control to stop, make the shot and take that split second to make sure the shot is better than what you're going to give it. Lobbing the puck and just drilling it at the goalie isn't enough. The shooter has to get the puck up and it's hard to make that transition. The player has to think and anticipate.

A player has to anticipate more than think. Some of the players think too much. They think so much they don't make the shot. They'll pass it to one teammate or another and never make the shot. Or, sometimes they'll come down the ice and bang, bang, they take the shot and the rebound gets knocked in. I don't see that as much. I see it evolve as the players get older and more experienced.

On the ice, everybody has a job to do and if they don't get the job done a goal gets scored against you. The biggest thing to be concerned about as a player is that you can't do too much. You have to orchestrate within what your responsibilities are on the ice. The one extra move or the one extra pass which a player will make spells doom for the execution. That's the E word that I use, and its not effort, it's execution. The bottom line is the job has to get done and if it doesn't get done you don't win hockey games.

We had a situation where we were down 1 to 0 the whole game, and all we had to do was continue to play our style and force Colorado to make a play. But we had our experienced defenseman of 3 years cough up the puck at the blue line and they came in and score on us. Now its 2 and 0.

The player who coughed up the puck comes back to the bench and says, "That was offside." But there was no whistle, and you always play until there's a whistle. The defenseman also went down on one knee and tried to keep the puck in the zone, which a player should never do on the point. It's worse than pinching along the sideboards. If you pinch off the boards, you leave the center open. A guy gets suckered to go to the boards and the other team's player flips it to his guy in the center, and it ends up being a two on one break.

My philosophy always has been if we lose, it's my fault. Some players will say the coach takes the blame, so it's no big deal. An experienced defenseman, a junior, once missed a flight to St. Louis, so I suspended him for two weeks. Could we have beaten DePaul with him in the lineup? We would have had a lot better chance, but the game is not all about wins.

Often I have to deal with the lack of respect some of these kids have for their own parents. I've mentored kids who are unhappy with their mom and love their dad, but when his dad steps on him, then he doesn't like that either. You try to help, but sometimes I am told I care too much. Imagine being told that by someone who's rudderless. That's your indictment, that you care too much. You know where these players weaknesses are and want to do something with those weaknesses and turn them into strengths.

Hockey and baseball aren't the only things that interest me. I always have had an interest in the Presidents of the United States. I was born in Illinois, the Land of Lincoln, our sixteenth president/ I've always liked history. President John F. Kennedy was assassinated when I was flunking an algebra test at Benet High School. I was around 14 years old when he was killed. I admired Lyndon Baines Johnson, JFK's successor. I even liked Woodrow Wilson because of the League of Nations. After the Treaty of Versailles was signed he tried to ratify the League of Nations, which was the forerunner of the United Nations. The US Senate didn't pass it and ultimately the world was drawn into World War II.

I am fond of Teddy Roosevelt, especially because I like his quote about being in the arena. 'Criticize me all you want, but get in the arena and get dirty,' he said. 'Get in there and see what you say, see how easy it is.'

I have many books in my library, which includes at least one book on every American president, but on Abraham Lincoln, I have 250 books.

I also collect presidential memorabilia. I have a Lincoln endorsement that's done in his hand. He made a man take a pledge in December 1863 and the endorsement is all in Lincoln's handwriting and signed by him. I have another Lincoln document, a presidential pardon, that's cosigned by Secretary of State William Seward.

The first presidential document I ever bought was a Woodrow Wilson document. I have signatures of many US presidents. A lot of the signatures are cut signatures from White House cards. I also have the signatures of all the twentieth century first ladies.

And I'm still collecting. My most recent acquisition was a ship's passport signed by James Madison and Thomas Jefferson, but Jefferson signed it in brown ink so you could see the TH and the Jeff, but the rest of his signature has faded. A couple of years ago I bought a ship's passport done in four languages, French, Spanish, Danish and English, signed in black ink by both Jefferson and Madison. My main consultant and advisor on these things is Daniel Weinberg of the Abraham Lincoln Bookshop in Chicago, a friend I've known for more than 25 years.

One of my documents comes from when a woman wrote a letter to James Polk from Tennessee, where he hailed from, and wanted his autograph. Polk died, so what Mrs. Polk did, in compliance with your request for my husband's autograph, I enclose this, and it was James K. Polk's signature, and a wax Polk seal validating the signature.

Books are also of interest to me. I recently acquired a book published in 1958 about the Montgomery civil rights march. The book is signed by Martin Luther King Jr. The inscription reads, 'To Roy, Best Wishes, Martin Luther King Jr.' I think it could very well have been to Roy Wilkins, who was head of the NAACP at the time and is listed in the book's index.

Martin Luther King Jr. was an icon of the 1960s, so having his signature, along with JFK's, Bobby Kennedy's signature on a book, and Barry Goldwater's signature is an accomplishment.

One of the nicest pieces that I have in my collection is a black and white United Press International photograph taken in August, 1959 of JFK, Jacqueline Kennedy and Richard Nixon. The photo is signed in ink by all three of them.

Other signatures include books signed by LBJ, a lot of Richard Nixon signatures, and also Gerald Ford and Ronald Reagan signatures. I also have one from our first president, George Washington, on a Revolutionary War requisition order.

I'm fond of telling people that baseball has always been my passion, and ice hockey is my job.

I was born and raised a Chicago White Sox fan. I didn't get the opportunity to go to a lot of games because my dad was working a lot of the time.

I played baseball in Little league, Pony League, Colt League, high school and college. I lettered as a freshman in college as both a first baseman and pitcher.

When Comiskey Park was torn down in Chicago in 1990, people were able to buy pieces of the old park. I was able to get bricks, a piece of the foul pole, some infield dirt, warning track dirt, and three chairs from the park. The chairs are bolted into my patio along with a railing and a light from the light tower at Comiskey. So today I can sit in old Comiskey Park every day if I wanted.

Coach meets Paula

Coach's first week as Lyons Township HS Varsity Hockey Coach with Brent Slezak and Rob Innes

Coach with mentor and friend Scotty Bowman

Bobby Hull attending an Icecats awards banquet

Brother Chet winning a heat race
at Santa Fe Speedway
September 14, 1974

Chet, Dad, Mom, Coach
Easter Sunday
April 18, 1976

Paula, Coach and Buster Brown

Brad Seger and Damon Simatos
Coach G's **MDA** buddies

St. Procopius College
"EAGLES"

1971 Midwest Intercollegiate Hockey Champions

Coach G (front row, second from left)
As pictured in the USA Hockey Hall of Fame

Coach as senior goalkeeper

As a freshmen with famed
midwest referee, Duke Gottschalk

Blues Portrait
1971

Watching
the Action

88

Coach with "The Chairman", long time friend, Jerry Reinsdorf
Owner of the Chicago White Sox and Chicago Bulls

Rex Allen Jr., "The Arizona Cowboy" Rex Allen, Coach

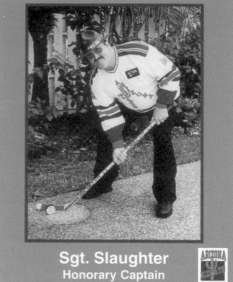

Sarge applying the
"Cobra Clutch" on Coach

Sgt. Slaughter
Icecat Honorary Captain

Mentor and Friend
NHL Player and Coach
Jim Roberts
5 time Stanley Cup winner

Tom Paciorek
Long time friend & Pole
MLB Player & Broadcaster

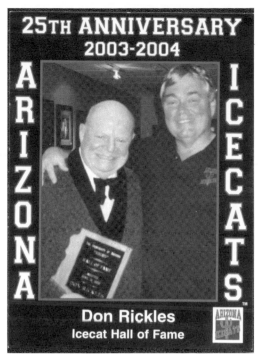

ARIZONA ICECATS

25TH ANNIVERSARY
2003-2004

Don Rickles
Icecat Hall of Fame

Coach – "Mr. Warmth" –
Manager Tony Oppedisano

Don Rickles
Icecat Hall of Fame
Inductee

Coach – Actor/Artist Buck Taylor –
and Brother Chet
at James Arness' 80th Birthday

Morgan Woodward
Legendary TV and
Movie Actor

Blackhawk Ab McDonald, Steven Kroll, Coach, Glenn Hall and Steve Aschburner

With the Late Jim Jalovec at Benedictine University Hall of Fame Induction 1997

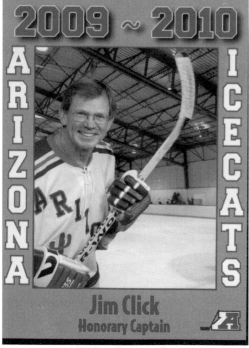

2009 ~ 2010

ARIZONA ICECATS

Jim Click
Honorary Captain

**"Mr. Tucson"
Tucson entreprneurial giant
Jim Click**

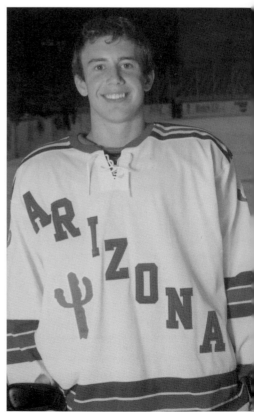

**Icecat Micah Kneeshaw
2007 - 2011**

92

Coach and "Mr. Goalie" with Lord Stanley's Cup

Coach wearing Glenn Hall's retired #1 Jersey

Coach ang Keith Magnuson in action at the 1994 Blackhawk Alumni/Icecat fundraiser hockey game

Coach and NHL Hall of Famer Stan Mikita after Blackhawk Alumni Game

**Coach with President
Ronald Reagan**

**Coach with President
Gerald Ford**

**Coach with U.S. Senator
Ted Kennedy**

94

Coach with legendary movie
directorJohn Landis who
directed Coach in
"Mr. Warmth –
The Don Rickles Project"

**Coach with Icecat honorary
captain Willie Nelson**

MR. McMAHON

1

**Coach with honorary Icecat
WWE Chairman, Vince McMahon**

**Coach with country music
icon Garth Brooks**

THE UNIVERSITY OF ARIZONA ICECATS
1985 NATIONAL COLLEGIATE CLUB HOCKEY CHAMPIONS

COACH
Leo Golembiewski

3	Dave Dougall
4	Mike Tovella
5	Joe Vogrich
6	John Lange
7	Steve Janakas
8	George Zabran
9	Tim Olson
10	Jack Adams
11	Bob Boldt
12	Bob Poole
14	Dave Ney
15	Mickey McConnell
16	Chris Pappas
17	John Eldean
18	Dino Paone
19	Joe Ventola
21	Jim Lindh
27	Bruce Wouters
29	Dave Jansen
30	Bryan McMillan

Coach and Paula

600th Collegiate Victory
January 9, 2009

96

13.
Friends

Pima County Sheriff Clarence Dupnik has known Coach G for more than 25 years and counts himself as a friend.

"Leo is one of a kind and unique in many respects," Sheriff Dupnik says. "First, he's a fierce competitor. He's responsible for ice hockey in Arizona — there was none of it before him. Leo built the Icecats with the labor of love and a lot of sweat and tears, with no help from anyone."

The sheriff sees another fierceness to the coach.

"He's also fiercely dedicated to the service of God," Dupnik says. "If he wasn't doing what he does, he would be a priest."

While Coach G likes to portray an image of a tough guy, Sheriff Dupnik thinks such a portrayal is meant to mask the coach's true demeanor.

"I don't see Leo as a tough guy; he's a big teddy bear," the sheriff says. "He's all about love and service. When Leo accepts kids into his hockey program he becomes their father, mother and brother."

The coach gets involved in his players' lives, says Sheriff Dupnik.

"Leo tries to give them direction in a way that makes them a better person, with better character," he says. "Leo tries to get them to be goal oriented and even helps them with their schoolwork."

But because of Coach G's fiery competitive spirit, he sometimes gets into difficulty.

"Leo had to beg, borrow and scrape to keep the Icecats program afloat — he gets no outside money except what he gets from the community," Dupnik notes.

"Consequently, he sometimes rubs people the wrong way. But he works diligently to get media assistance for the Icecats and usually he's successful, but sometimes media egos get in the way."

Yet it's Coach G's educator background that seems to come through most strongly, Dupnik asserts.

"He's a fantastic teacher and incredible communicator with a tremendous sense of humor," the sheriff says. "Leo could have made a very good living in a variety of fields because he's had several opportunities to do other things, like being the athletic director of a college, but he's dedicated himself to the Icecats."

Coach G can also be quick on the trigger, even with his friends. Sheriff Dupnik tells of playing golf with Leo during one of the Icecats annual golf outings.

"I was always a fan of Baseball Hall of Famer Leo Durocher, who was known as Leo the Lip," says Dupnik. "Well, I called Leo 'the Lip' during that golf match and he didn't talk to me for the rest of the day. I never called him that again."

In the end, it all comes down to what Coach G does with the kids on his team.

"Leo takes these kids and treats them as his own, as all good coaches do, but I think he does it much better," the sheriff says. "He has a higher graduation rate at the University of Arizona than any other other sport, he makes sure the kids go to class and that they're prepared, in spite of no assistance from the University. He makes sure the Icecats are a treasure to Tucson."

Dave Dougall played for the Arizona Icecats as a defenseman from 1983 to 1987 and has been working with Coach G in a coaching capacity since 2006, so if anyone knows Leo Golembiewski's coaching moves, it's Dougall.

Dougall remembers his first contact with Coach G at the Iceland arena where the Icecats practiced.

"The coach asked me, 'Are you any good?,'" Dougall says. "I told him, 'I'd like to try out,' and he responded to me, "But are you any good?' I told him he'd have to judge that."

Dougall would make the team and indeed turn out to be a good hockey player, serving on the coach's national championship team in 1985. He was 17 when he made the team, much younger than some of the other players who were 24 and 25.

"The rules were the same for everybody, but the coach takes the younger guys under his wing to help them develop as both a player and a person," Dougall says. "He likes to give more leeway to the older guys who have more experience in life."

One of the requirements for playing on the Icecats team was that a player couldn't neglect his studies, Dougall points out.

"The players who were good students also worked hard on the ice because that's the style of hockey we played," he says. "Coach spent a lot of time working with us individually on the ice, and as you progressed, you were expected to perform more."

Dougall became co-captain of the Icecats during his third year.

"Coach said the guys who were more character people where the ones who became captains and co-captains," Dougall notes. "They were the guys who were supportive of the program, were team players and could see the bigger picture."

Dougall believes that Coach G's methods are very much focused on the psychology of his players and learning what makes them tick.

"He's always trying to get the most out of individuals and maximizing their potential," Dougall says. "Coach is not an X's and O's kind of guy — he has a certain style that he wants us to play."

That style involves stretching the opposing team the length of the ice and making opposing players work as hard as possible.

"Most people tend to be lazy and take the easy way out," Dougall observes, "so this strategy works well. We make the opposing players skate hard and then we get opportunities."

Dougall continues, "We try to set everything down deep, behind the net and take the puck into the corners. We don't want to see our guys cutting from the blue line toward the center of the ice, which is a transition area. We don't want them passing the puck there, we want to see them skate it and carry the puck in. We've won a lot of games that way."

Dougall characterizes himself and Coach G as opposite personalities.

"I'm reserved and he's outgoing," Dougall says. "Coach can sometimes be abrasive, and he doesn't let many people in. He has the expression on his face that looks like he's not overly friendly. And when he's upset, you don't want to go anywhere near him."

The reason for Coach G's demeanor, Dougall believes, lies in the fact that coach doesn't want to show any weaknesses, and yet has a passion for his players and the game of hockey.

"He will defend his territory and make sure everyone holds up their end of the bargain, from the players to the hotel front desk clerk when we're on the road," Dougall observes.

Yet, Coach G can be as charming as ever, when he chooses to, says the associate coach. In a work environment, Coach G portrays a very different personality — very gruff.

"You're not sure you want to ask him a question some times," Dougall says. "He wants you to keep your mouth shut and do your job. But as the season rolls on he lightens up. Still, he scares the crap out of you."

Many people perceive Coach G as intimidating because of that gruff demeanor, yet are curious about what makes him tick.

"He's definitely a person of interest because he's been here so long, but also because he's so fiery," says Dougall. "He used to throw things, kick water bottles and knock sticks over."

In fact, Dougall stresses that Coach G has a good sense of humor.

"He's especially good with the one-liners, particularly during his locker room speeches," Dougall says. "He can keep it light when he wants; it depends on if he senses the team is down."

Coach G also will poke fun at himself at times to let everyone know they're on the same side.

"He mocks himself as the person everyone loves to hate," Dougall says, "the dumb Pole from Chicago and whether or not he really knew so many National Hockey League players and coaches. The kids are unsure how to take him sometimes, whether they should be laughing or not. There's a lot of looking around to see if it's okay to laugh."

Yet it's the success of the Icecats program that drives Leo Golembiewski.

"Leo buys sodas, sandwiches and rolls of tape on his own for these kids and they don't realize that it's him doing it," Dougall says. "Coach comes in early and sets up the locker room. He cleans up too, but the kids might think it's the water guy or the stick guy doing this stuff. Besides that, he's always the last one off the bus and into the restaurant when we're on the road. He's always making sure he's providing for the team."

The Icecats is one of the last club programs to charge a player fee. Most other college club hockey teams have a couple of thousand dollar fee to make their program work. The first year the Icecats charged a fee — $500 — was 2009. However, the team (that is, Coach G himself) still provides, pads, equipment and uniforms for the players.

Coach G's biggest strength?

"It's his perseverance," says Dougall. "He built the foundation for the Icecats and then continued to build the team. He's been successful with the more than 400 players who have come through the program — coach has molded them all into teams over the years."

Coach G's biggest weakness?

"I think it would be coaching with his heart," Dougall admits. "Coach puts his heart and soul into everything, and sometimes that lets him down. It can be his biggest frustration, but he probably wouldn't have gotten this far if he wasn't like that."

John Dadante is the voice of the Icecats — the announcer at home games and on the radio.

Yet Dadante's relationship with Coach G goes back to 1980 when Dadante was a drama teacher and Coach G was an American Government teacher at Salpointe Catholic High School in Tucson. The two teachers knew that many students would try anything to dodge when they weren't prepared for class, but Dadante and Coach G were slicker than the students.

"We shared a common interest in that we wouldn't let a student get out of one class to attend a different one," Dadante says. "That was known as the 'GD' rule. If a kid wanted to get out of my drama class and go to Leo's American Government, we wouldn't let it happen; we got along well in that way."

Dadante says that Coach G's sense of humor is like Leo himself — blue collar.

"Maybe it's because of his Catholic upbringing," Dadante says. "He reminds me of the altar boys I grew up with in Cleveland, guys with devotion; Leo still has that, but there's two sides to him — the religious side and the hockey side."

At Salpointe, Coach G regularly played practical jokes.

"There was a very short nun, Sister Mary Peter, at Salpointe who Leo used to call 'Sister Yoda,' probably because of her short stature and the black-and-white habit she wore," Dadante points out. "Leo used to move her mailbox nameplate up to the top rung of the stack of mailboxes so she couldn't reach it. He has a good sense of humor."

Dadante likens what he and Coach G did at Salpointe as having similarities.

"There's a lot alike between what I did in theater and he does coaching," Dadante says. "With both theater and coaching, you look at the person's size and stature, and with me, I watch them read the script, but Leo watches them put on skates to see what they can do. Actors or players, they're working at similar roles."

Dadante notes that Coach G always proclaimed that success was something the kids on his team did; if there was no success, it was because of something Coach G did wrong.

"I always got the best interview from Leo after a loss," Dadante says. "Leo always said that he gives the kids the wins and he takes the losses. For Leo, if a player didn't take a shot, it's not his fault, its because of the direction he received from the coach."

Dadante points out that years ago players readily bought into Coach G's philosophy that family comes first, then academics, and only then, hockey.

"These days it's social life first, and it drives the coach crazy," Dadante notes. "His style of coaching is the other way and it's difficult to change. Leo coaches the same way he did 20 years ago, the same way Scotty Bowman coached him. That's his history."

He continued, "Scotty Bowman, Glenn Hall and Jimmy Roberts were his mentors, and they all talked and played a different style of hockey. Today it's a different mind game from back then, so it's tough being a coach these days."

Dadante says that Coach G is very concerned about people.

"If you have a story, Leo is willing to listen," Dadante points out. "If it's enough of a tear jerker, you've got him. One day Leo called me and asked if I was all right because he had a dream about me the previous night and wanted to be sure I was okay. I had quit my Icecats job the year before, but my situation had changed and Leo offered me my job back."

Dadante has done radio broadcasts of the Icecats games for more than a dozen years and the public address announcing at home games for about 17 years.

Coach G doesn't react to situations in the manner in which ordinary people do, Dadante maintains.

"He may be a reactionary, but his heart is huge," Dadante says. "I've seen him react to people close to him where he goes out of his way to help them. You don't talk to Coach G on game nights because then he has his game face on. It was halfway through my first season before he spoke to me during a game."

The perception of Leo Golembiewski ranges from devotion to dislike, Dadante believes.

"The media types think he's arrogant because he holds his club hockey team to NCAA standards, New York Yankees-style," Dadante says. "But for the season ticket holders and other fans, Leo is the Icecats, no ifs, ands or buts. After 32 years, there's no other club team in the country that deserves the respect the Icecats have missed. I dare anybody to come up with a team outside of the University of Arizona that has lasted that long and run in the red, yet been as successful."

Donn Ricketts has known Leo Golembiewski since 1987 and admits he's only called him by his first name a few times.

"I either call him 'Coach' or 'Coach G' because that's his title, who he is," Ricketts says.

Ricketts was intrigued by the idea of ice hockey in the desert, especially after learning the Icecats had won the national championship a couple of years earlier. He attended most of the Icecats home games that year and then became a corporate sponsor for his three companies.

"One of the things I like about his program is the way he runs his team," Ricketts says. "He not only coaches the sport, but also teaches a good bit beyond the game as well, which is fitting, since he also used to be a teacher."

Ricketts, who became a member of the Icecats board of directors, notes that Coach G's philosophy of education as his team's first priority, then family, and finally the game itself, has had the effect of a graduation ratio in the 90 percent range, where other sports programs are lucky to be in the 60 to 70 percent range.

Describing Coach G's character, Ricketts says the coach is straightforward, direct and honest.

"Leo will not pull his punches, whether he's talking to a potential sponsor or one of his players," Ricketts points out.

Yet Ricketts believes that people who don't know the coach will perceive him as arrogant, stubborn and brash.

"If saying what is on your mind is arrogant," Ricketts notes, "then it's the problem of the person doing the perceiving."

As for being perceived as brash, Ricketts thinks most brash ventures turn out to be good moves and that progress generally is not made by sheepish individuals.

Ricketts admits, however, that stubbornness may be a Coach G trait, but only in a good fashion.

"The coach won't buckle under because he knows his players and how things should be run," Ricketts observes.

"For the coach to come to the desert with a dream of a hockey team, to build it into a winning team and continue it for more than 30 years is quite remarkable," Ricketts says. "During those years he had opportunities to go with other colleges and professional teams, but he chose to stay in Tucson with the Icecats. That's dedication."

Jim Click, president of the Jim Click Automotive Team and often called "Mr. Tucson" because he's such an entrepreneurial giant in the region, says, "In Tucson, for years and years, when you think about hockey, you must think of Leo and what he did for the University of Arizona Icecats. He was the Icecats and he continues to encourage our youth to enjoy ice skating and ice hockey."

Click says nearly every year, his company "enjoys a huge promotion for our employees by going down to the arena and watching an Icecats hockey game. They were always fun and competitive. For two years, we had our major Christmas party at the Tucson Community Center and then went to an Icecats hockey game."

He continues, "They remain fond memories and we will always be grateful to Leo for what he has done for hockey in the city of Tucson, and for what he continues to do for the young players. He brought world-class hockey to our city. Thank you, Leo."

14.
A Good Friend of the Coach

Jimmy Roberts began his hockey career in Canada in the 1950s under then-Peterborough Petes coach Scotty Bowman. He later turned pro with the Montreal Royals, moving to several different teams in the ensuing years. His first NHL activity was with Montreal in 1963 and four years later in 1967 he was selected as a first pick by the expansion St. Louis Blues.

Roberts spent four and a half years with the Blues until he was traded to the Canadiens, where he had won two Stanley Cups in the 1960s with the team. It would be 1977 before Roberts found himself back with the St. Louis Blues for another season, in 1977-78, before he retired.

Roberts first met Leo in 1969 when Roberts was captain of the St. Louis Blues.

"Leo was invited to our training camp in 1971 as a goalkeeper," Roberts says. "We hit it off and we've stayed friends ever since."

When Coach G wasn't chosen for the Blues team, he went on with his life, coaching hockey and baseball around the Chicago area while Roberts continued his NHL career.

"We never got together other than when he came to town to play, or later, when I came to Tucson to visit," Roberts says, "but we stayed in touch since those first days."

Roberts believes that Coach G is successful because of the confidence he shows in himself.

"Leo is not afraid to stick his neck into the wringer for what he believes in," Roberts says. "Look at what he's done with his hockey program. He's been very successful in developing the team and developing the kids."

Roberts calls Coach G's attitude "bulldoggish because he sticks with what he thinks and wanted to do. Leo always has loved coaching young kids and giving them the opportunity to succeed in hockey and in life."

While professional league hockey coaches are compensated very well, Roberts maintains that Coach G "did it the hard way" with the Icecats.

"What he's accomplished speaks very well of him as a person who has given a lot of his time freely," Roberts observes.

While some people who don't know Coach G will see him as being a bit pushy and abrupt, Roberts thinks those perceptions don't reflect the actual man behind the image.

"I see the side of him who's a friend and a person who has helped a lot of young players get into the game," Roberts says. "Leo's been very dedicated to hockey and to educating kids."

Although Roberts thinks Coach G has slowed down a bit in recent years, he still believes the coach is as thorough as ever.

"The last few years Leo has stopped spending a lot of time on the ice with his players, but before that, he was on the ice all the time," Roberts notes. "He would always ask me and other hockey acquaintances about programs and drills to run, and continually was interested in accumulating more information about how to be a better coach and relate to his players."

Roberts says that it's difficult to coach players who aren't very accomplished at the game, yet Coach G plugs away at it and has been successful.

"He's so serious about the Icecats program and always is copying good ideas and working them into his program," Roberts adds.

While Roberts admits that he's disappointed that Coach G never left Tucson and took a higher paying and more noticeable coaching job in either college or professional hockey, he says it doesn't matter.

"As it turns out, Leo has made a good program for his kids in Tucson for all these years and it shows in his dedication," Robert says. "Leo has sacrificed quite a bit with not a lot of monetary gain for himself, but that only shows his determination and dedication. I'm pleased to have been a part of Leo's career as a friend and feel very good about how he's made hockey available to these kids and still helped get them a good education."

15.
A Really Tough Guy

Sgt. Slaughter is an actual tough guy.

He's been a WWE champion wrestler for 30-plus years, was inducted into the Wrestling Hall of Fame in 2004 and still can scare the crap out of most people. Yet for all Sgt. Slaughter's accomplishments as a tough guy, he admits that he admires Coach G's tough guy routine.

"I think Coach G has to have a hard ass kind of attitude as a coach because he's responsible for all of the players," Sgt. Slaughter says. "He's like their father as much as being a coach because they're away from home and a lot of them are still young kids — 17, 18 and 19 and probably away from home for the first time. He has to be responsible for their well being."

Sgt. Slaughter, (actual name, Robert Remus), encountered Coach G for the first time in an unorthodox manner, yet one suited to his WWE wrestling career. Coach G tried to smash him with a chair.

"We were at a golf tournament to benefit the Boys and Girls Club of Santa Cruz County in Southern Arizona," Sgt. Slaughter says. "They asked if there were any questions and I wanted to know what the first, second and third prizes were. They told me and I asked my team which ones they wanted. Everyone got a chuckle out of my brazen attitude."

Once all the questions from players were answered, Sgt. Slaughter made an announcement to the group.

"There's going to be a battle royal behind the clubhouse after the tournament," he announces, but was surprised by what happened next.

"I felt this chair on my back and as I turned around I saw that it was coach," Sgt. Slaughter says with a smile. "I had never met him before, but here he is trying to hit me with a chair like we might do in wrestling around the apron of the ring. Coach says to me, 'Battle royale, you said. That means no holds barred.' I immediately knew I would like coach."

After the tournament, Sgt. Slaughter and Coach G sat together and Leo peppered the wrestling champion with question after question about wrestling.

"He told me about watching wrestling when he was a kid and how much he enjoyed it," Sgt. Slaughter says.

Later Sgt. Slaughter would become an honorary captain of the Icecats.

"It was a real thrill," he says. "I was living in Naples, Florida at the time and coach sent me an Icecats jersey. I put it on — in 100-degree heat — grabbed a hockey stick and went outside by my pool and had a photo taken for his hockey cards. When I saw all the big names of people who had been Icecats honorary captains, it blew my mind that he knew all those people."

A little-known side of Coach G is that he's something of a practical joker, according to Sgt. Slaughter.

"Coach has a great sense of humor and pulls stunts on me all of the time," he says. "When I arrived in Tucson this trip, he takes me to my hotel room to make sure everything is okay. It was completely dark when we walked in and we kept turning on switches until the place was lit up."

Sgt. Slaughter continues. "I was pretty bushed and went to sleep at 2 a.m. At 7 a.m., someone is pounding on my door and I thought it was coach. Then the phone started ringing as I get up to answer the door. I head to the phone and it stops, but the door pounding starts again."

When Sgt. Slaughter finally got to the door, a manager was there, asking if he was all right. Coach G had put the Sarge in a room for the disabled that had panic switches on the wall to alert hotel staff if the person needs help. When coach and the Sarge were slapping on light switches, they triggered the emergency alarm that lit up a red light outside the room.

"The hotel staff was worried that something had happened to me," Sgt. Slaughter said, "but it took them five hours to find out. The joke was on me, but things like that happen all the time with the coach."

Sgt. Slaughter sees himself and Coach G as kindred spirits.

"I never would have made it in professional wrestling if I hadn't developed a character," Sgt. Slaughter says. "I started as Beautiful Bobby Remus, with long blonde hair, tie-died costume, and pink and purple boots. It wasn't me and didn't work. When that red light came on (on the television camera) I would freeze, and was so nervous I developed hypertension."

He solved the problem by developing the Sgt. Slaughter character, partly because he was a staff sergeant in the U.S. Marine Corps.

"Both coach and I get into character in a way," Sgt. Slaughter says. "I become a character when I get into the ring and coach becomes a character when he's doing anything related to hockey. The tough guy is the character he portrays when he's on the ice and when he's a coach dealing with his players."

16.
More Friends Speak Out

Hugh Anderson, OSB (Order of St. Benedict), served as Abbot of St. Procopius Abbey in Illinois for 18 years and as chancellor of Benedictine University and the Benet Academy from 1985 to 2003. He remembers Leo at what was first St. Procopius Academy (the high school) and later St. Procopius College, as a history major working under the hard-minded head of the history department, Christian Clepeckta, OSB.

"Father Christian was a tough person and Leo had to write his senior thesis in order to graduate," Abbot Anderson says. "Leo had to be a serious student, otherwise he would never have gotten through the program and received a positive response from Father Christian."

Abbot Anderson remembers that whenever he talks about Leo, the first think that comes to mind is hockey.

"Leo lived and breathed hockey," Abbot Anderson says. "He was part of our team as goalie at the college and played very competitively."

There was one particular irritant that got under Leo's skin during his college hockey games, though, Abbot Anderson noted.

"Some of the students would sit behind the net and someone would blow a trumpet, which would drive Leo up a tree," Abbot Anderson says. "They weren't doing it to annoy him, but rather to rouse the crowd, but it drove him wild. He never told me why, though."

Abbot Anderson adds that it was a priest who was the lips behind the trumpet.

"Father Tim Navin was the one who blew the horn at the games," Abbot Anderson says. "He couldn't play the horn so he just made as much noise with it as he could."

Trumpeting notwithstanding, Coach G continues to be a strong supporter of the abbey, Abbot Anderson pointed out.

"He is a good friend and supporter of the abbey and the college," Abbot Anderson says. "Everyone here calls Leo 'the coach.'"

Bill Carroll, PhD, president of Benedictine University, sees Coach G a couple of times a year and classifies him as "a generous donor to the university," which now has approximately 10,000 students.

"I came here as president in 1995, so I never knew Leo when he was a student here, but it's clear that his love of the Benedictines is phenomenal," Carroll says.

Carroll notes that Leo was part of the first class of Hall of Fame athletes in 1997 at Benedictine University.

"He is an honest, caring guy, a good man who loves the kids he works with," Carroll says. "Leo is a kind, gentle guy, yet he still can be a bull in a china shop. He takes no prisoners and lets you know exactly where you stand."

Carroll believes that ingrained in Leo's personality is that of a coach — sometimes soft and sometimes hard, but all the time working with you.

"He can come across as gruff at times, and then he might seem like a country bumpkin-type of person," Carroll says. "He doesn't wear coats and ties well, that's not who he is, and he can scare some people, but that's not intention, yet he smiles when he does. He's brutally consistent — there are no gray areas with him — it's all black or white."

Leo doesn't fit into most of the boxes that people try to fit him into, Carroll maintains.

"He's a bright, intelligent guy who doesn't fit any stereotypes," says Carroll.

For instance, after Leo moved to Tucson, he acquired a horse and boarded it at a stable not far from his home.

"Leo's relationship with that horse, Buster, was very close," Carroll says. "He visited that horse every day and brought it carrots as a treat. I don't think Leo ever rode Buster, but to this day he's never told me why he had not."

Whenever Leo returns to the Chicago area, he spends time at the University.

"Coach G never tells you when he coming," Carroll says. "He just knocks on your door and says 'hello.'"

Visiting aside, Carroll says he knows where Coach G is aiming for a final resting place.

"He's told me he wants to be buried either in our St. Procopius Abbey graveyard here or Holy Trinity Monastery in St. David, Arizona," Carroll says.

Jim Dewhirst of Decatur, Tenn., is both a banker and lawyer and has lived in Chicago and San Francisco. He's been an official with USA Hockey since 1980 and has served as referee in chief for the southeastern district since 2001.

"I played on the first two teams that Leo coached at Lyons Township High School," Dewhirst says. "I met him the summer before my junior year of high school on rented ice, which was a big deal at the time, to ice skate inside in the summer. My friend told me this goaltender was going to be there who had been at the St. Louis Blues hockey camp."

Dewhirst continues, "Leo played goal for awhile and then played forward. I have never been checked harder than I was by Leo — good, solid, clean checks. This was the summer of 1972 and I had no idea that he's to be my coach in a few months."

Dewhirst says that revenge can be sweet, because he was able to score a goal on Leo during that summer ice hockey game.

"He hates it when I say that," Dewhirst says. "He always trivializes that goal."

But Dewhirst classifies Leo as a very good goaltender.

"A few times during the years I played for him he put the pads on and got into the goal," Dewhirst says. "Leo is extremely competitive."

During Dewhirst's junior year with Leo as coach, the team won 18 and lost one, losing the championship game. His senior year, the team played in two high school leagues and won 61, lost one and tied one, winning the championship in both leagues.

"Leo had a way of making us play better as a team," Dewhirst says. "We beat teams that had better talent than we had. Leo could be a sonovabitch — looking back, it seems like we did nothing right and anything we did, we could do better."

Coach G likes mind games, Dewhirst believes, and that's what gets the best performance out of his players.

"After every game we won, he would come into the locker room and rip into us about what we didn't do right and how we would have to get better," Dewhirst says. "But the one game we lost that year, he walked into the locker room and we thought we'd get ripped up royally. Leo never said a word, except that 'practice is tomorrow. See you then.'"

Leo also had some quirks as a coach, Dewhirst remembers.

"He was not a fan of the officials and let them know it loud and long," Dewhirst says. "And he would do some strange things. One game when we were not playing very well and the officials seemed to be against us, he called a time out in the middle of the second period. Coach gathers us at the bench and starts telling us the story of Goldilocks and the Three Bears in a very animated way."

The referees began getting nervous and one approached Coach's bench, Dewhirst notes.

"When the ref comes over, Coach gets upset and says, 'I'm telling this story right now.'" Dewhirst says. "Then he tells us to go out and play hockey. What he did was take his foot off the pedal and tried to pull us out of the framework we were in and into another one. We ended up winning, but the method was really bizarre."

While Coach G likes to put forth a hard image of a "hard-assed sonovabitch," says Dewhirst, "he really is not like that."

When Dewhirst was refereeing in the late 1980s and early 1990s, he often would bring a crew of officials to Tucson from Los Angeles or San Francisco to officiate a Friday or Saturday night game.

"Many times after the game, Leo would ask us if we were getting something to eat and would tell us where they were going so we could have dinner with him," Dewhirst says. "After getting ripped during the game by Leo, those officials who didn't know him would encounter him as a friendly, charming gregarious guy. They always had a great time at dinner with Leo."

Dewhirst believes that Leo has mellowed somewhat over the years.

"He was pretty fiery when he was young," Dewhirst says. "He told me that coaching college is very different than coaching high school hockey because there are so many more distractions in college."

Dewhirst notes that in high school, the players were thinking hockey all the time, practiced or played six days a week and were pretty much a family.

"Leo says its harder to get college kids to buy into that way of thinking and playing," Dewhirst points out. "I think he has to use a lot more psychology with them. Where he used brute force personality with us, with the college kids he has to think more about how to get the best out of his players."

Roland Hemond, special assistant to the president and CEO of the Arizona Diamondbacks in Phoenix, served as general manager of the Chicago White Sox from 1971 to 1985. Hemond says he first met Coach G in Tucson during a White Sox spring training game.

"He's an excellent baseball fan for a hockey man," Hemond says. "He has a fine knowledge of baseball as well as hockey, so I can see why he's such a good coach."

Hemond characterizes Leo as "a really friendly guy who goes out of his way to know a lot of other baseball people. And in return, they respect the job he does and enjoy his company."

Hemond believes there's a mutual respect amongst sports people, because of the necessary teamwork, recruiting and organization being so similar across different teams and sports.

"Leo always comes across as a real gentleman," Hemond says. "The tough guy comes out when he's coaching, but you have to be tough to play that game. The challenge is that to be successful with his program, he has to be a tough guy, so the success he's had is certainly to his credit."

Tony Oppedisano, road manager for comedian Don Rickles, met Coach G about eight years ago at the Stardust Casino when the coach attended a Rickles show where Larry King's wife, Shawn, was doing the opening act.

"Coach had been on the Larry King show prior to that night and Larry gave him a big welcome," Oppedisano says. "But mainly Leo came to the Stardust because he had always been a big fan of Don's."

While Oppedisano could see that "he was chomping at the bit to meet Don, I could tell he was a very sincere, gently guy," he says. So Oppedisano, who's worked for Rickles for 18 years, brought Coach G backstage to Don's dressing room after the show.

"When I introduced him as 'Coach G,' Don teased, 'What is this, a spelling test? Leave it to Tony O. to introduce a guy named Coach G," Oppedisano notes. "Then Don jokes to Leo, 'You're Polish.' Leo answers, 'Yes.' Then Don asks, 'What do you do?' and Leo says he's coach of a hockey team in the desert. Don's response — 'Only a Pollock would be the coach of a hockey team in Arizona.'"

Yet while Rickles made jokes with coach, both he and Oppedisano would become aware of Coach G's dedication to the Icecats team for the University of Arizona.

"It's always been the focus of his existence," Oppedisano says. "He's always trying to figure out a way to keep the money coming in to keep the team going."

Oppedisano thinks Don Rickles and Coach G share personality traits.

"They are both guys who come on strong," Oppedisano says. "Don is a great humanitarian, and a loving, caring guy. Coach G is the same way. They're both all bark and no bite."

And both Oppedisano and Rickles are appreciative of what Coach G has done for them.

"Don and I are members of the UA Icecats Hall of Fame," Oppedisano says.

But it's what Coach G gives to the people he encounters that impresses Oppedisano so much.

"Leo has a huge heart — he's very giving and loyal," Oppedisano says. "He mentors people and takes great pride in watching kids succeed and then go on in life an reach what plateau they're destined to reach."

Jerry Reinsdorf, owner of the Chicago White Sox and the Chicago Bulls, met Coach G at Comiskey Park, years before Leo made the move to Tucson.

"Leo is a native of the Chicago area, and like so many other Chicagoans, you may be able to leave the area, but you will forever remain a fan of our sports teams," Reinsdorf says. "That's how I grew to know Leo best, through his continued passion for all things Chicago, especially the White Sox."

Reinsdorf notes that so many White Sox fans have relocated to Arizona, that the team's spring games often have the feel of being at home on the South side of Chicago.

"Leo just chose to beat a few decades to the punch by moving to the warm weather earlier in his life than most snowbirds," he points out. "But like pitchers and catchers reporting on the first day of spring training, we could always count on seeing Leo each March."

Reinsdorf says that when the White Sox held spring training in Tucson, "Leo was a frequent visitor to our camp and I doubted he missed many Cactus League ballgames. We used to laugh about how many of the members of our front office had Icecats hockey pucks sitting on their desks, all because of meeting Leo. And if you know Leo, you know his life's true passion is hockey."

Reinsdorf believes Coach G accomplished much in Tucson.

"I admire him a great deal for making ice hockey work in the desert," Reinsdorf says. "Coach G enjoyed more than three decades of hockey success in perhaps the least likely of locales — sunny Tucson. His many accomplishment speak for themselves — coaching 32 seasons, posting 634 wins and raising a National Championship trophy in 1985 — the very same year a special Chicago sports team lifted the Lombardi trophy."

From Reinsdorf's viewpoint, Coach G has achieved great things with the Icecats, but at the cost of plenty of hard work.

"I can't begin to imagine the thousands of hours Leo spent on the ice, growing and promoting ice hockey in Tucson," he says, "and I am certain his experiences have given him a lifetime of stories that can entertain from blue line to blue line and probably beyond."

Tom Paciorek, a long-time friend of Coach G and a former Major League Baseball All Star and broadcaster, jokes that even though he's known Leo for 30 years, because he, too is Polish, it took him only 10 years to pronounce his name correctly, but he's still working on the spelling.

"I do know his name means 'pigeon' in English," Paciorek jokes again, adding that "Wimpy is his (Paciorek's) nickname, given to him by Tommy Lasorda"

But in a serious vein, Paciorek says, "I've never met an individual more dedicated to the advancement of young men, in both athletics and life. Leo has been a great mentor to all the players he's coached, and a father figure who's not afraid to discipline his guys, and at the same time, love them unconditionally."

Paciorek continues, "His efforts at the University of Arizona not only translated into victories, but more importantly to the development of fine men. Leo's unique style reminds me of 'ole Blue Eyes, the great Frank Sinatra, who sang *I Did It My Way*. Best of luck, Leo."

Morgan Woodward, a motion picture and television actor, says that during his 50 years in the movie and TV business, he's received some strange fan mail.

"I once received a letter from a guy who's name I could not pronounce — Golembiewski," Woodward says. "There were enough letters there for three names and I thought it might be a fan from Warsaw, Poland, but no, this guy began by telling me he is the coach of an ice hockey team in Arizona."

Woodward continues, "Ice hockey in Arizona? I thought, this guy must be nuts, but continued to read and by golly, I started to believe him. That letter began a long friendship with one of the most extraordinary men I have known. I need not expand on his accomplishments because when you read his remarkable story, you will not only agree with me, you will be greatly rewarded."

17.
Thoughts From Players and Coaches

G. Gary Gould has known Leo Golembiewski since 1972 when they both were coaching high school hockey teams in the western suburbs of Chicago, Illinois. At their first meeting, when each of their teams had a 22-0 record, Coach G's team scored the deciding goal and won the game 3-2.

"We go to shake hands after the game and he walks right past me," says Gould. "No problem, I think, I will shake his hand in the locker room area. Again, he ignores me, so I say to myself, 'Okay, the hell with you Leo.' We did not speak to each other for nearly two years."

The other side of the story is that when Gould's team won for the first time against Coach G's high school hockey team, Coach G stopped Gould at mid-ice and gave him a bear hug. Not long after that, Gould says that Coach G came up to him at the hockey arena and said he wanted to buy Gould lunch.

"One thing led to another and we have been good friends since then," Gould says.

Yet there's another side to Coach G that few people would expect.

"Leo invited me to his high school hockey team's banquet," Gould says. "Imagine the look on his players' faces as I, the enemy coach, took a seat at the head table. And then imagine the look on the faces of my players when Leo and Paula attended our banquet."

Gould continues, "It's a small insight into who Leo is, and a large insight in what Leo does. He cares about others and he shows respect to those who might be perceived as the enemy."

Still, Gould has known Coach G for more than 36 years and during that time they have had their differences.

"One minute we can be standing toe to toe, shouting at each other, and the next minute we are talking normally and the situation is resolved," Gould says. "Leo wants to be the boss, but he is man enough to admit when he is wrong and will accept another's point of view."

Gould says that Coach G, both then and now, is a very focused individual.

"His team, the game and the situation are all he is interested in," Gould points out. "You do not want to get in his way when he is getting ready for a game, or during the game, or directly after the game. His game day demeanor is 'Stay out of my way.'"

Continuing, Gould notes, "You basically do not approach him unless he asks you a question. So he is many times perceived as a very gruff and impersonal person by those who do not really know him, but to those who know Leo, he is a very religious and caring person who will do anything he can to help his family, players and friends."

And Gould thinks that Coach G's ability to make friends is part of his successful personality.

"To people in his hockey world, he may seem standoffish and tough to approach, but for those people not connected with his hockey team, he is a very intelligent and caring person," Gould says. "One cannot have as many friends in the sports and entertainment world as Leo does without having that special, 'I really do care about you and what you do' attitude. Leo is not one to give up easily, and once he gets it into his mind to get to know someone, he goes all out to meet them."

Micah Kneeshaw, a forward on Coach G's 2007 to 2011 teams, thinks that as a coach, Coach G isn't that difficult to figure out.

"He's very direct and to the point, and he lets you know what he wants to get done," Kneeshaw says. "On the ice, he acts big and tough because he's working with a bunch of college kids who think they are at the top of the universe. But he's stern and tells them, 'I don't care what you think, this is what's going to happen and this is the way it's going to get done.'"

Kneeshaw says he always gets the sense that Coach G knows exactly what is going on with everyone on his team at all times.

"Each person seems like they have their own personal closeness with the coach," he says. "The coach is there for them all the time and knows what they're going through and if they need help. When he's on the ice, he's working; when he's off the ice, he's a friend."

Kneeshaw calls Coach G's style powerful.

"Everything with the coach goes down deep — there are no ifs, ands or buts," Kneeshaw notes. "Every drill or practice is always done at full speed — there's no finesse, it's just getting the job done."

The coach also has an exceptional grasp of the finer details of the game, Kneeshaw believes.

"He brings up details about shooting that I've never thought of," Kneeshaw says. "My skating is probably my strongest thing, what got me on the team, and I thought I had it down to a 'T' and couldn't improve it, but here's the coach saying 'You're doing it all wrong,' and 'You need to improve your stride and come up with more power.' The coach goes through the mechanics of it with you, so even if you don't know how, he tries to show you what you should be trying to do."

In the final analysis, Kneeshaw says he counts Coach G as a close friend.

"I consider him a really close friend," Kneeshaw says. "I didn't pick up on that until he started coaching me on a personal level, but I learned he really knows more than I ever though he would have and he's comfortable sharing it."

Sally Sloan's late son Bill played for Coach G from 1981 to 1984 and she's seen a change in the coach from the years when Bill played hockey for him, an Icecat Hall of Famer, his #2 jersey was retired by the Icecats.

"Coach G always was tough with the kids, but he's not as tough with them as he used to be," Sloan says. "There's a softer side to him now. Bill always saw Coach's softer side and that's probably why they were friends too."

At Bill's memorial service, Coach G told a story about using the Sloans' motor home to transport the team to away games. On one trip to California, everyone was asleep in the motor home except Bill and Coach, and when the song, Pina Colada, came on the radio, Bill began singing and trying to dance in the driver's seat to keep awake.

As Coach G spoke about the event, Sloan's daughter cued up an MP3 version of the song on her mobile phone and put it over the speaker. Sloan says everyone had a good laugh.

Sloan thinks she knows why Coach G has such a tough exterior personality when many people say he's much softer inside.

"He's a teacher, an educator," she says. "He trying not only to teach hockey, but also to teach how to be a good person. Most of the time, I think he's successful because the kids respond to him."

Jarett Goodkin, an Icecats Hall of Fame goalie, played for the Icecats from 1985 to 1989. He says when he first met Coach G in 1984, he was "just a voice on the other end of the phone when he called our house to speak with my father, who was the faculty advisor for one of the college club hockey teams from Southern California. I finally met Coach G in person after I had the unusual opportunity as a high school student to play goal for that club college team against the Icecats. We lost to the Icecats 6 to 5 that night, but apparently Coach G liked what he saw because he had good things to say about me when I spoke with him."

Goodkin says that since Coach G is a former player who made it all the way to the St. Louis Blues' organization, he understood only too well the obstacles American players were up against.

"So he built a program from the ground up for American players like me," Goodkin notes. "By the time I joined the Icecats in 1985, they had just won a National Championship and were drawing several thousand fans a game. The team paid for our travel to away games on planes and buses, and we stayed in hotels just like the Division I teams."

However, the Icecats still were a club team and didn't have the money to pay for scholarships and equipment, except for pants, gloves and helmets. Besides money, the biggest thing missing at the time, Goodkin observes, was a good practice and training facility. The first two years Goodkin played for the Icecats, the team practiced at the Iceland Bowl and Ice Arena.

"Words cannot really describe Iceland," he says. "The rink was only 117 by 70 feet (a regulation rink is 200 by 85 feet)," Goodkin says. "It only had one side with plexiglass above the boards, while the other three walls were brick, not quite as forgiving on a player's helmet and head as plexiglass. By the time a player would wind up to take a slap shot, he was practically standing on top of the goal crease, and the blue line was a few stick lengths away. If you had any fear of getting hit in the head, you either got over it or quit playing."

Goodkin says that while Iceland was a challenge for players, it was many more times difficult for Coach G.

"Besides the size of the arena, he had to worry about the corner where the pipes did not work, causing holes and ruts in the ice," Goodkin points out. "I have no idea how Coach came up with the drills that seem to make it all work, and from what I remember, no one ever got injured in practice. For those times when we needed a bigger sheet of ice, he would stick us on a bus and take us to Phoenix. Of course, we ended up having to skate late at night and didn't get home until the early hours of the morning."

Coach G managed the Iceland Ice Arena at the time and had to deal with two Zamboni ice resurfacing machines — one from the 1950s and the other from the 1960s.

"The one from the 1950s only turned to the left, which was completely opposite of the way you were supposed to do the ice," Goodkin says. "Coach was the only one daring enough to drive that one. The rest of the rink employees, including me, were too worried about crashing it."

Goodkin says the 1960s Zamboni caught fire at least twice and the drive shaft had to be rigged because the chassis had to be extended after the engine was replaced. Coach G's brother Chet somehow kept the Zamboni running. When it finally gave out, Coach G found a used Zamboni on the East coast.

"Unfortunately, the exhaust from that Zamboni was so potent, we would have to leave the big Zamboni doors to the outside open, which allowed in the heat," Goodkin says. "I still remember going straight home after work to take a shower because I smelled like a car's exhaust pipe. I once crashed the conditioner (the part that goes on the ice), bending it like a pretzel. I though Coach might get really angry with me, but he seemed just to take it all in stride."

Besides the issues with the Zambonis, there were even bigger problems with the pipes and compressors.

"The pipes underneath the ice constantly leaked, which meant we had to fill the system with glycol on a regular basis," Goodkin says. "Some of the other pipes were clogged, causing holes and ruts in the ice. The pipes were only part of the problem. The compressor had already been rebuilt once and we had to pump oil in it on a regular basis. It was not an easy task and we always had to guess how much it needed."

Goodkin continues, "I remember the day I came into the arena to find the ice melting. There was oil over the floor and the compressor sounded like someone hitting metal with a sledgehammer. Needless to say, the Iceland era was over."

Despite the loss of Iceland, Coach again figured out how to put it all together for the team, Goodkin notes. "There was dry land training that we did on the ramps outside the U of A's McKale Center, bus trips to Phoenix time and again, and finally at the Tucson Convention Center after they put the ice in when they had no other events scheduled. Somehow, Coach was still able to make the Icecats successful on the ice."

Goodkin says that during his time at the U of A, he and Coach G became very close friends.

"In some ways it was and is a very strange combination," Goodkin observes. "I am 18 years younger, Jewish and the son of a physician. He is a devoted Catholic and the son of a truck driver. However, we shared a common love of goaltending and hockey. Using his coaching and goaltending experience, he transformed me from a young high school hockey player into a fairly successful college goaltender."

Goodkin adds, "During my four years as an Icecat, I played as many Division I games as a back-up Division I goaltender. Coach even had Gary Unger, who was coaching the Phoenix Roadrunners, take a look at me during one of the Roadrunners' practices."

Yet there was more to the relationship than only hockey, Goodkin maintains. The two built a solid friendship. Goodkin became a friend of the whole Golembiewski family and lived in a duplex owned by Coach's mother.

"I often helped her with odd jobs, fixing things and painting the duplexes she rented out," Goodkin says. "I was treated as one of the family."

Goodkin notes that Coach took him on several recruiting trips where he had the opportunity to see many American landmarks, such as the St. Louis Arch, Mount Rushmore and Lincoln's birthplace.

"The extra bonus was visiting those places with Coach because he's a former American Government teacher and knows so much about our country's history," Goodkin says. "I also saw many professional baseball games at Comiskey Park and Wrigley Field, and had the opportunity to meet many pro baseball players because Coach did baseball scouting on top of being a hockey coach."

After graduating from the University of Arizona, Goodkin became the team's assistant coach.

"That's when I learned about the team's financial struggles and Coach's tireless efforts to keep the team skating," Goodkin says. "Over the years our friendship has survived. Coach stood as one of my groomsmen at my wedding in September 2000, and we continued to stay in touch. I am grateful for his friendship, which very much played a part in the person I have become today, and wish him success in the future."

18.
Friends Across the Country

Steve Aschburner of Chicago is a journalist who went to high school where Coach G coached high school hockey in LaGrange, Illinois.

"I knew of him when he was coaching high school and was a junior writing for the school newspaper covering the hockey beat," Aschburner says.

Aschburner lost touch with Coach G after the coach moved to Tucson and established the Arizona Icecats, but says he got reacquainted with coach over the last three years.

"I did my homework on his success in Arizona with the Icecats, and thought that if the United States Hockey Hall of Fame is meant to honor people who honor the sport, then Leo is a good candidate with his many successes in high school hockey and with the Icecats."

Leo also is a college hockey pioneer with the National Collegiate Hockey Association, from 1983 to 1991, and with the American Collegiate Hockey Association to the present.

Accordingly, Aschburner put together an application, consulting with the coach on dates and background, and submitted Coach G's name as an applicant for the Hockey Hall of Fame.

"Leo planted a hockey flag in Tucson a long time ago and kept it alive and well through today," Aschburner says. "In his early coaching days, he was an ultra-confident and nearly the most cocky guy around, but these days even Leo might admit there's a potential chink or two in his armor."

The selection process for the Hockey Hall of Fame, located in Eveleth, Minnesota (www.ushockeyhall.com) is handled through USA Hockey in Colorado Springs, Colorado. Inductees are announced every summer.

"Of all the people who should be in the Hockey Hall of Fame, someone like Leo who has built the game and encouraged the sport surely should be represented," Aschburner says.

Actor, stunt man and painter Buck Taylor thinks Coach G's confidence is one of the strengths that could get him into the Hockey Hall of Fame, but also believes it's what endears coach to his hockey players.

"The coach is actually a softie, but he wins the confidence of the kids through his own strong beliefs and through discipline," Taylor says. "Coach wins you over really easily because he is so since and honest."

Although Coach G may portray himself as a gruff, unapproachable, tough guy, Taylor believes that's all a façade.

"Coach G is in it for the passion of what he lives," Taylor says. "He's actually a very unassuming guy."

Jim Ferguson of Tucson, a broadcaster, movie reviewer, friend of Coach G and fellow Chicago White Sox fan, met the coach more than 30 years ago when he was teaching at Salpointe Catholic High School in Tucson.

"After he created the Icecats, he appeared on my television talk show on ABC Channel 9 many times," Ferguson points out. "Over the years, I've learned that he's driven and hardworking, a good Christian and trustworthy."

Ferguson says that one of the coach's strengths is his generosity.

"Often I've seen him give Icecat hockey pucks to kids during baseball spring training games in Tucson," Ferguson says. "And many times he has given me Icecats gifts to give to my celebrity star interviews in Hollywood, which they enjoy very much."

Ferguson notes that he and Coach G often were the first two people in line to get tickets to Chicago White Sox spring training games.

"We're both sad the team has moved its spring training to Glendale (Arizona)," Ferguson says, "but those games in Tucson were always so interesting because coach would always have stories to relate about the umpires, players and owners."

At one time, Coach G has been reported as saying, "If I hadn't become a hockey coach, I would have become a Benedictine monk."

Father Henri Capdeville, OSB, the prior of Holy Trinity Monastery in St. David, Arizona, a Benedictine order monastery, says that Coach G was a strong support to him when he took over directing the monastery upon the death of Father Louis Hassenfuss, OSB in 2001.

"Leo was very generous in supporting the community by inviting us to his home and also to be with his team, the Icecats," Father Capdeville says. "As I got to know him better he was a strong support for me. We started raising funds together for both of our entities — him for the Icecats and me for the Holy Trinity Monastery."

Father Capdeville notes that Coach G thought of becoming a Benedictine monk when he was much younger.

"Leo is a man of faith and is very fond of the way our faith is expressed through the Benedictines," Father Capdeville says. "He has been very generous in allowing us to sell baked goods at Icecats games. At one time the authorities wouldn't let us into the game to sell our goods, but Leo got to the big boss and convinced him in no uncertain terms to let us in. If Leo believes something is right, he will fight for it."

Father Robert G. Tamminga, pastor of St. Francis de Sales Catholic Church in Tucson, has followed the exploits of Coach G and the Icecats for some time.

"When I became pastor of the church 25 years ago, I was excited to learn that Coach G was a member of the parish to which I was newly assigned," Father Tamminga says. "I contacted coach, we went to breakfast and began a friendship that continues to this day."

Father Tamminga describes Coach G as a teddy bear who puts forward a grizzly bear exterior.

"He is one of the most fiercely loyal and motivated people that I have ever met," says Father Tamminga. "There is not much that is part-way or half-way with the coach. He expects and demands the best from himself and his hockey players, loves his country, and loves his family unconditionally."

Father Tamminga notes that many people perceive Leo to be a great coach, but brusque and abrasive.

"I would say that a great number of his detractors are simply jealous," Father Tamminga observes. "The more one gets to know Leo, the more he is seen to be a man of deep integrity and passion. Certainly he can be brusque, but always in the context of reaching for the highest goals."

Father Tamminga points out that when Coach G talks about his hockey players, he speaks with the affection and concern, much as a father would.

"Often in conversation, I hear him speaking about his strong emphasis on the scholastic education and strengthening of the moral character of his Icecats players," Father Tamminga says. "Leo's team members are training to be men of character — responsible citizens and not only hockey players."

Father Tamminga calls coach's wife Paula "the love of his life," and thinks that coach is sometimes surprised that she puts up with his rough public exterior and stubbornness.

"This is a marriage which is tried and true," the pastor says. "Leo is a valued, loyal and beloved friend of mine and I love what he's done for Icecat Hockey and the many young men he's help form, as well as his dedication and devotion to our church and his wry sense of humor."

19.
Roommates

If anyone, besides Coach G's wife Paula, know him relatively well, it would be his former roommates at St. Procopius College (now Benedictine University). Those would be Bill Calzaretta, Greg Munie and Alan Barc.

Calzaretta, the former executive director of suburban campuses for De-Paul University and current director and associate professor at DePaul's School of Public Service, has the greatest amount of time spent with the Coach, having attended St. Procopius Academy for four years with Leo.

"I met him in 1963 when we were both high school freshmen and remember him as being a little insecure during his first year," Calzaretta says. "But before long he got his feet under him and began developing his strong personality."

After four years as a fellow high school student with Coach G, Calzaretta and Leo both went on to St. Procopius College, where they roomed together as freshmen and sophomores.

"If you ask the high school and college colleagues of Leo to describe him, they would say what a pain in the ass he was," Calzaretta says. "Leo always had a reverence toward Don Rickles (the comedian) and Glenn Hall (the NHL hockey player). Leo also used to do an imitation, constantly and irritatingly, of Pat Piper, the Chicago Cubs announcer. It was like getting hit with an iron fist in a velvet glove."

While Leo seemed like "a very sensitive guy" to Calzaretta, his roommate says Leo also was very much into sports, but also into helping people.

"The image that he projected was not the real Leo," Calzaretta points out. "Now the people know him as the coach, the hard guy, which is the persona he created. Still, he's a very accomplished person and a visionary in what he did with the team (the Icecats)."

Calzaretta believes that Coach G has created something bigger than life with the Icecats in Tucson.

"He's the architect of that," Calzaretta noted. "While he needed to have that hard guy image as it was expected, he's not really a hard guy. That's his mechanism of security and safety, and the image that he wanted to project, which he did very well."

Calzaretta says he has always admired Leo's hockey interest, but also his similar interest in the religious life too.

"I went into the monastery, and while Leo came close to doing so, he didn't, but he still lives that life," Calzaretta noted.

Calzaretta was a Benedictine monk for two years, taking simple vows, but decided not to pursue that religious life, so was never ordained as a priest and left the monastery. He later attended graduate school, earning a Ph.D in psychology.

Coach G's former roommate thinks Leo is a complex personality.

"He's a bit insecure and needs to be reassured that he is doing well and is successful," Calzaretta says. "But he's a genuine person, professional, skilled and a motivational coach. Still, he wears two masks — his goalie mask and the persona mask of a hard guy."

Leo's roommate for the second semester of freshman year, and all of his sophomore and junior years, was Greg Munie, currently an independent contractor for the non-profit IPC, an electronics group of 5,000 companies around the world developing standards and training methods.

Munie remembers that St. Procopius College was "in the middle of farm fields so it was a pretty quiet area, meaning people at the college hung around together." Munie met Leo at college through someone who had attended St. Procopius Academy and suggested he room with Leo and Bill Calzaretta because the rooms held three students.

"Leo introduced me into several things — hockey, because there wasn't much hockey in Decatur (Illinois) where I'm from; baseball, where he turned me into a Chicago White Sox fan; and professional wrestling," Munie says. "There were no phones or televisions in dorm rooms back then, and the only television was in a lounge area. So Leo introduced me to the wrestlers of the time — Dr. X, Dick the Bruiser, Mitzu Arakawa and the Crusher."

Munie also remembers Leo introducing him to cows.

"His cousin had a dairy farm in Wisconsin and the monastery (St; Procopius Abbey) had a dairy operation that it was getting rid of," Munie says. Leo would bring me across the street and educate me about the cows."

Munie notes that the three roommates also named their dorm room and themselves.

"Bill Calzaretta was the Mouse Man, I was the Rag Man, and Leo was the Great God of the Nets," Munie points out.

Leo talked a lot to his roommates about hockey and especially his idol, goalie Glenn Hall.

"We went to some Chicago Black Hawk games with Leo when Glenn Hall was supposed to be there but never got to meet him because he didn't make the trip (from St. Louis)," Munie says. "Leo talked a lot about him and knew a lot of people on the Black Hawks."

Munie remembers Leo as being a "pretty serious guy with whom you could talk about anything. He had a strong Catholic background and was a very good listener."

Munie notes that as a goaltender, Leo had to be willing to take a few shots, but thinks that Leo's laser focus and lack of a temper helped him in that regard.

But one goaltending chore turned out to be a difficult proposition for Leo, Munie says.

"I recruited him to play goalie on our soccer team," Munie notes. "But the size of the goal was five times as big as the hockey goal he was used to defending, so Leo wasn't used to the very wide lateral movement. But he gave it his best shot."

20.
The Leo Golembiewski Celebrity Golf Classic

The first Leo Golembiewski Golf Tournament debuted at the El Conquistador Golf Club in Oro Valley, northwest of Tucson on Labor Day weekend in 1985.

At that time, the Muscular Dystrophy Association held a series of golf tournaments throughout the year in Tucson to raise money and help fund MDA's efforts. Local MDA members approached Coach G and asked him to put his name on a final tournament that wrapped up all the MDA-related golf tournaments held throughout the year in Tucson. Coach G gladly accepted the request and the Leo Golembiewski Golf Tournament was born.

Coach G had been involved in the MDA Telethon locally since the inception of the Icecat hockey team. The Iceland Bowl and Ice Arena at 5915 E. Speedway Blvd. would stay open throughout the 21 hours of the MDA Telethon each year. Coach G and the Icecat players would annually participate by answering phones and taking pledges during the Labor Day Telethon broadcast on Tucson's KGUN-9 TV.

Coach G became a member of the Tucson MDA Executive Committee and eventually was honored to meet and talk with the legendary Jerry Lewis. He also would meet and become friends with two notable boys stricken with Muscular Dystrophy — Brad Seger and Damon Simatos.

Court and Cathy Seger, Brad's parents, say their son looked forward to Coach G's annual golf tournament for the MDA.

"He attended the tournaments and thrilled at being driven around the course in a golf cart, getting the opportunity to talk with the golfers, especially the celebrities," Court Seger says. "Along with Damon Simatos and Nick Parker, also suffering from MD, the kids were called the 'Three Amigos.'"

Court Seger was involved in the tournaments too, helping sell sponsorships, putting up signs and working on communications.

Brad Seger also delighted in attending Icecat hockey games.

"He would not miss a game," Court Seger points out. "Brad especially liked when the players would get checked into the boards right in front of him. He had signed sticks from each Icecat team between 1989 and 1993, the year he died."

Sam and Maria Simatos, Damon's parents, say their son benefited from Coach G's generosity from 1985 until his death in 1993.

"During that period, Coach G involved Damon and other children in activities and events, that because of their disability, they may not have had the opportunity to experience," Sam Simatos says.

Maria Simatos notes, "From golf tournaments to Icecat hockey games, Coach G made Damon an active participant, which cheered Damon and gave us some of our fondest memories."

THE WINK OF A LIFETIME

On September 7, 2011, as I ascended from Petco Park's Field Level, my eye caught Augie Nieto and his wife Lynne.

They were heading for a pre-game ceremony where San Diego Padres CEO, Jeff Moorad was to recognize the Muscular Dystrophy Association's Augie's Quest. A charity that gives 100% of funds raised to ALS (Lou Gehrig's Disease) research.

Since Augie's diagnosis six years ago, more than $29 million has been raised to find a cure to this horrific disease.
Meeting Augie and Lynne was an awesome experience. Their courage and determination is truly inspiring and I gave them a 600th victory puck and our golf tournament shirt.

As I talked to Augie and Lynne, Augie wrote to me that it was an honor to meet me and along with other things told me his nephew was a hockey goalie.

As I touched his arm to say goodby and thanks, he winked back at me, an experience I will never forget for the rest of my life!

For more information about MDA- Augie's Quest go to www.augiesquest.com

21.
A Call to the Hall

By Steve Aschburner

Hockey is huge in Eveleth, Minn., a frosty, no-nonsense town of about 3,800 folks on Minnesota's Iron Range. And they let you know it the instant you drive into the city's center. There it is: 107 feet long, weighing more than 3 tons in all its wooden glory. What had always been known as The World's Largest Hockey Stick sits right downtown, a tribute to the hockey tradition in the region and the sport's impact on so many participants and residents.

Manufactured by the Christian Brothers stick factory in Warroad, Minn., a couple hundred miles northwest of Eveleth near the Minnesota-Manitoba line, the Bunyanesque exhibit is said to have enough wood for 3,000 regulation-sized hockey sticks and is twinned with a 700-pound puck that might also be the largest in existence. Wait, check that: Eveleth's pride and joy now gets described as "The World's Largest Free-Standing Hockey Stick" because up in Duncan, British Columbia, they now have an even bigger one fastened to the side of the community center. Or "centre," as they spell up there.

No matter. Even with the world's second-largest stick, Eveleth believes it takes a back seat to no other American burgh, big or small, when it comes to hockey. It is, after all, home to the United States Hockey Hall of Fame, a museum and shrine to the sport's deepest American roots. Dedicated in 1973 and located out near the interstate, the USHHOF was an attempt to add some Cooperstown cachet and chamber-of-commerce appeal to a town that definitely is off the beaten path.

Billed as the "National Shrine of American Hockey," the US hockey hall is a smaller, grass-roots alternative to the more celebrated Hockey Hall of Fame in Toronto, which honors top NHL performers and personnel. The USHHOF is dedicated to ice hockey contributions – allegedly at all levels – from south of the Canadian border. A total of 148 players, coaches, builders and administrators have been honored, with museum exhibits dedicated to the 1960, 1980 and 1998 (women's) U.S. Olympic teams, to coach Herb Brooks and to other highlights – look, it's an early Zamboni! – owing to American skills, competition and ingenuity.

There is a strong Minnesota and Eveleth influence at the Hall, too, thanks to players and coaches with local ties such as Mark Pavelich, Frank Brimsek, John Mariucci, Willard Ikola, John Mayasich, Sam LoPresti and Doug Palazzari among the enshrines. So many, in fact, that one could argue that the USHHOF belongs in Eveleth.

And Leo Golembiewski belongs in the USHHOF.

That was the premise, anyway, held by more than a few of Coach G's supporters and by two longtime friends dating back to his high school days coaching the Lyons Township Lions. Both Jim Jalovec, who starred on the LTHS squad for Golembiewski, and Steve Aschburner, who covered the team for the student newspaper, had known the coach for close to 40 years in the western Chicago suburbs when they brainstormed the idea to nominate Golembiewski for enshrinement at the USHHOF. More than that, though, they had witnessed the long and impactful arc of his career.

They had seen it all: The shaping of boys into young men not just on the ice but off. The instruction in both hockey fundamentals and advanced strategies, with life lessons tossed in free of charge. The creation and nurturing of a program from scratch, in the unlikeliest of places: Tucson, Ariz. Success in the form of more than 600 intercollegiate victories, numerous tournament appearances and titles and a laudable graduation rate for his Icecats players. A lifetime given to the sport, all in the U.S., as a pioneer in a hockey-deprived region of the country and a builder in providing opportunities – at his school and others – for talented players to continue in the sport beyond high school.

Jalovec, a successful entrepreneur based in Naples, Fla., wrote an impassioned letter of recommendation to the USHHOF selection committee on Golembiewski's behalf in 2008. Here is an excerpt:

"I don't know how the man does it, but he created a program which draws thousands of fans to home game. I have seen the Tucson Convention Center full, with over 5,000 screaming fans, with my own eyes. [And] he and his team get little or no help from the university. Leo had to create an organization that funded the whole operation. ...

"What I want to stress is Leo's impact on my life through lessons taught on the ice. Leo gave me the confidence in myself to make me truly believe there wasn't anything I couldn't do if I put my mind to it. ... I really love and respect this man. I don't personally know of anyone who has had such a positive im-

pact on our sport. He brought hockey to the desert long before "The Great One,"
Wayne Gretzky, did."

Aschburner, a sportswriter with SportsIllustrated.com at the time, was the one who submitted the formal nomination form for Golembiewski's consideration. In a letter that accompanied the application, he wrote:

"His achievements, in sheer victories and winning seasons, rank him among the most effective secondary-school and intercollegiate coaches in the country. … Eight years before [Gretzky] and one year before the "Miracle On Ice" USA team galvanized interest in the sport again, the Arizona Icecats were building a following, one relocated player and fan at a time.
"Hockey rarely has had a more driven and dedicated advocate."

The nomination was made in March 2008. In August, the USHHOF announced its Class of 2008: NHL stars Brett Hull, Brian Leetch and Mike Richter, along with NCAA women's star Cammi Granato. The first three were good enough to merit enshrinement at the "big" Hall in Toronto, so the selection committee seemed to have passed up, in Golembiewski, a chance to honor U.S. contributions at the seed level.

No matter. Nominees, by USHHOF rules, receive consideration for three years before having their names set aside. Golembiewski still had two more bites at the Eveleth apple. And the list of endorsements, testimonials and recommendations was growing:

"At one time Leo might have said that the highlight of his career was attending the St. Louis Blues training camp, but now he knows that the highlight has been starting a hockey program in Tucson. … If you can improve the direction of a young person, what a great job you have done! Leo has done that."
-- Hall of Fame NHL goaltender Glenn Hall, Golembiewski's mentor

"I have seen his work up close from my participation in his banquets there and from my position as an 'honorary captain' of the team one year. … His efforts on behalf of the sport and the creation of the Icecats program truly are laudable. He has made it possible for many young, talented hockey players to receive solid educations while seeing a part of the United States they might not otherwise see. He has set high standards for those young men on the ice and in the classrooms, and he has done this out of his love of hockey and his desire to pay forward some of the many benefits that our great game has given to him."
-- NHL legend and Hall of Famer Bobby Hull

"I cannot think of any person who has devoted more time, energy or passion to the game of ice hockey. He singlehandedly envisioned, developed and implemented a club hockey program at the University of Arizona. Through his efforts, a rabid fan base for ice hockey in Tucson has been developed, and its popularity continues to increase. In additon, his efforts have resulted in thousands of Tucson youth being exposed to ice hockey and developing an interest in participating in this great sport."
-- Jim Livengood, former director of athletics at the U. of Arizona

There were more, from people with NHL connections who have known Golembiewski for decades to players who recently graduated after spending four formative years on the Icecats.

Then in the summer of 2009, the verdict came down again: No go. Tony Amonte, Tom Barrasso, John LeClair, Frank Zamboni and that '98 women's Olympic team made the cut but Golembiewski did not.

The nomination packet was freshened up again for 2010. More victories by the Icecats to enhance their coach's record, more tributes from hockey people who knew and appreciated his work. But a few comments from back in 1994 by the great Scotty Bowman – the NHL's winningest coach and another mentor to Coach G – spoke as loudly as any about the younger man's contributions. And Bowman made these comments at the time of Golembiewski's 300th coaching victory, back when the Icecats had realized less than half of their success with him:

"   I told him that he should go and try to start [the Arizona program]. If you have a dream about something and then you don't do it, then you end up thinking about it for the rest of your life.

"Hockey will survive because there are coaches like Leo Golembiewski who are dedicated to the game. Leo has given his whole life to hockey and I'm happy to be here to honor him."
-- Scotty Bowman

In February 2010, Jalovec, Coach G's friend and former player, was tragically killed in a helicopter crash on a relief mission to earthquake-torn Haiti. An energetic advocate for the coach's inclusion was lost. And when the Class of 2010 was announced and formally enshrined in October, once more Golembiewski was not invited. The inductees were Art Berglund, Derian Hatcher, Kevin Hatcher, Jeremy Roenick and Dr. V. George Nagobads.

Word has since leaked out from those close to the selection committee – the process is handled now by USA Hockey in Colorado Springs – that there may be a bias against – or, to use a less-loaded term, a lack of appreciation for – the club hockey level of intercollegiate play. Some committee members are said to feel that, if a team isn't varsity (that is, funded and fully embraced by the school's athletic department), it offers up an inferior product.

To which those familiar with Golembiewski's work counter: Club, schlub.

Tell it to the players who pay their own way to participate, rather than coasting on scholarship money with full access to school facilities. Tell it to Golembiewski and his coaching staff, who must divide their time between the sport and the endless challenge to stay financially afloat. Tell it to folks at the Tucson rink on a Friday or Saturday night, cheering as if these were the Blackhawks, the Kings or the Canucks. Tell it to the parents who pitch in to help their kids, then talk glowingly upon graduation about their Icecats experience.

Better yet, tell it to the U.S. Hockey Hall of Fame in Eveleth. www.ushockcyhall.com Nominations for the Class of 2012 will be taken soon and Golembiewski's name again will be submitted. He will be in the queue, waiting again, with hopes that he soon can take his rightful place in the shrine.

Afterword
June 15, 2011

What was I thinking?

Tonight, the death of my father reached 35 years — he never lived to see the Icecats. Tonight, the Boston Bruins won the Stanley Cup for the first time since 1972.

In 1972 I started my hockey coaching career, thinking I would dedicate my life as a teacher and coach, taking my education up to that point and life's experiences to help young people. As it has evolved, I've coached 18 seasons of baseball and 39 years of ice hockey.

In my sports room at home, I have a photograph of "The Goal," scored in 1970 by Boston Bruins' defenseman Bobby Orr. He's in flight — horizontal to the ice — with St. Louis Blues' defenseman Noel Picard in the slot with my friend, hero and mentor, Glenn Hall, backed into the net. The photo is autographed by Bobby Orr, who in my view, is a player who altered the great game of hockey more than anyone else with his skating, shooting, passing and offensive-mindedness. Glenn Hall also signed it, "To Leo. I showered before Bobby landed. Thanks for everything. Sincerely, Glenn Hall."

What was I thinking? Foregoing even my dream of coaching in the National Hockey League, with a few opportunities presented, I started teaching and coaching American hockey players in the game I learned from Glenn Hall, Bobby Hull, Stan Mikita, Jimmy Roberts, Lynn Patrick, Sid Abel, Al Arbour, along with my coaching mentor, Scotty Bowman, who I've known since 1969. No, I'm not name dropping. It has been people like this and others who have influenced my coaching style with the commitment and dedication to the players in both of these sports I love.

What was I thinking? It's being a "hopeless romantic," or as my wife Paula says, maybe, perhaps, just "hopeless."

What was I thinking? I wanted to give back to the American, Canadian and European players what I learned from some of hockey's greatest.

139

Well, after almost 1,000 victories in hockey — 634 with the Icecats and 32 years after founding the organization, I found myself without a team to coach. Is there a problem with the "new type" of player — those who are allowed to wander in this age of hype and sound bytes? What happened to hard work, honesty and loyalty? What about ethics? I guess I am that "old type" of player.

Watching the Bruins hoist Lord Stanley's Cup — again, as every year — a tear comes to my eye. How awesome! I dreamed since I was 12 years old of getting my name on that Cup — an unusual dream for an American kid from Chicago in the 60s. What might have been if I listened more earnestly to those who influenced my coaching career?

What was I thinking? One can dedicate one's self for more than financial gain. Try to teach young people about those "intangibles" in the "hockey handbook." Not coaching just to win a few hockey games, but winning in life. We all know that life's a climb, but it's worth the view.

Teacher, coach, mentor — anti-drug and anti-drinking — sort of against the grain. What are they and the critics thinking?

Bruins players tonight spoke of "hard work" and "discipline." That is what I'm made of. That constitution is what I always tried to instill in my teams. These same convictions, I will inspire again.

That's what I'm thinking!

Coach G

Appendix A — Icecats Player's Handbook

Purpose: These are the player guidelines, expectations and the team philosophy.
(You are expected to know the contents of this handbook.)

Thoughts About Icecat Hockey
• Playing for the Icecats should be viewed as a privilege.
• Use common sense in your academic, as well as your hockey participation.
• A mature attitude is needed on and off the ice. Go to class and work hard in practice.
• Team goals should be put above personal goals.

Needed Intangibles
• Discipline
• Dedication
• Sacrifice
• Commitment
• Responsibility
• Honesty
• Loyalty

Goals
1. Team spirit and a winning attitude
2. A strong work ethics
3. Win a national tournament
4. Play up to all competition
5. A 2.75 accumulative team academic GPA (Grade Point Average)

Success, both personal and team success depends on:
1. Family
2. Academics
3. Icecats — your hockey career

Keys to Success in All Life Stages
• The building blocks to lifetime success are discipline, dedication, sacrifice, responsibility and commitment. Hockey is simply a vehicle to your present and future lifelong development.

Hockey is physical and psychological. It is not only speed and coordination, and agility and endurance, but your adaptability in regard to those four attributes.

Characteristics of a Good Student – Hockey Player
• Attitude
• Control
• Hard work
• Intensity
• Intelligence
• Consistency
• Poise
• Mental toughness
• Aggressiveness
• Second effort
• Judgment
• Leadership
• Self discipline
• Loyalty
• Honesty

Ways of Succeeding As an Icecat
1. Preparation. It must be both physical and psychological, which means sacrifice, commitment and responsibility.
2. Knowledge of style. This means executing and anticipating hard work, which takes discipline.
3. Achieving. We do this for both ourselves and for the team. It takes dedication and a belief in the team concept.

Icecat Playing Style
• We like to use the fast break, play to the headman, use position play and position ourselves wide and deep.
• Teamwork. This requires a strong work ethic, working together as teammates, drawing from each other's strengths, and working to overcome both team and individual weaknesses.
• Excelling. When we excel, we ensure both personal success and team success.

Making Things Easy

1. Classroom performance. Attend classes regularly, study diligently and keep up with assignments.

2. Practices. Work hard, be attentive, be cooperative and show intensity.

3. Games. The team goals always supercede an individual's goals.

4. Attitude. Be mature and positive toward your teammates, the coaches, staff, board of directors, fans and university instructors.

5. Problems. If you have academic, hockey or personal problems, see the coach. We are here to help you. Do no keep things to yourself.

Our Team

- What goes on with us is our business only.
- Keep all team business in the "family."
- Do not discuss team concerns with non-team members.
- Get to know your teammates and learn to respect them as individuals.
- We will all laugh, hurt, cry and sweat together.

Leo Golembiewski Biography

- Head Coach and Founder (1979) of the Arizona Icecats
- Native of Lyons, Illinois
- Bachelor of Arts in History, 1971, Benedictine University, Illinois
- Master's degree in Education, 1981, University of Arizona, Tucson, Arizona
- Lettered 4 years in ice hockey, two years in tennis and one year in baseball at Benedictine University
- Attended St. Louis Blues Pro Training Camp, 1971
- Attended St. Louis Blues Rookie Camp, 1972
- Married former Paula Parz, October 15, 1977
- Teacher, American Government, 1979 to 1985, Salpointe Catholic High School, Tucson, Arizona
- Member of Muscular Dystrophy Association Executive Committee (Tucson)
- Recommending scout for the Cincinnati Reds, 1979-1989
- Played goalie for the Chicago Blackhawks Alumni in Muscular Dystrophy Association charity game against the Arizona Icecats, 1994. Wore Blackhawk Alumni jersey No. 1, which was retired in 1988 in honor of Hall of Fame goalie and Coach G's mentor, Glenn Hall, who told radio listeners, "There is no one else I would allow to wear that No. 1." Coach G notched the 10-6 victory and recorded an assist on a goal by Hall of Famer Stan Mikita. The game was coached by Hall and Reg Fleming. Game 2 was played in December of 1995.
- Hall of Famer and the National Hockey League's winningest coach, Scotty Bowman, comes to the Tucson Convention Center, to honor Coach G's 300th win.
- Co-founder, National Collegiate Club Hockey Association (1983 to 1991)
- Co-founder, American Collegiate Hockey Association (1991 to present)
- President of the American Collegiate Hockey Association, 1995 to 1997; Vice President of Division 1, 1991 to 1993
- Member of Rocky Mountain Intercollegiate Hockey Association, 1981 to 1984
- Commissioner of the Pacific Intercollegiate Hockey Conference, 1985 to 1989
- Sponsors an annual golf tournament for charity (1985 to the present)
- Works with the Pima County (Arizona) Sheriff's Department Drug Abuse Resistance Program
- Enjoys presidential history, political science and the Chicago White Sox

- Inducted into the Pima County Sports Hall of Fame in 1996
- Inducted as a charter member of the Benedictine University Athletic Hall of Fame in 1997
- Wins the 600th game as Arizona Icecats Head Coach in 2009
- Nominated to the USA Hockey Hall of Fame in 2008

University of Arizona Icecats
Year By Year — 1979 - 2011

1979 – 1980	5 wins, 3 losses, 0 ties
1980 – 1981	Rocky Mountain Intercollegiate Hockey Association Regular Season and Playoff Champions 17 wins, 5 losses, 2 ties
1981 – 1982	Rocky Mountain Intercollegiate Hockey Association Regular Season and Playoff Champions 12 wins, 5 losses, 2 ties
1982 – 1983	Rocky Mountain Intercollegiate Hockey Association Regular Season and Playoff Champions 16 wins, 5 losses, 0 ties
1983 – 1984	Pacific Intercollegiate Hockey Conference Regular Season and Playoff Champions 2nd Place National Collegiate Club Hockey Tournament 15 wins, 5 losses, 0 ties
1984 – 1985	Pacific Intercollegiate Hockey Conference Regular Season and Playoff Champions 1st Place National Collegiate Club Hockey Tournament 28 wins, 3 losses, 1 tie
1985 – 1986	Pacific Intercollegiate Hockey Conference Regular Season and Playoff Champions 4th Place National Collegiate Club Hockey Tournament 27 wins, 5 losses, 0 ties
1986 – 1987	Pacific Intercollegiate Hockey Conference Regular Season and Playoff Champions 2nd Place National Collegiate Club Hockey Tournament 12 wins, 4 losses, 2 ties
1987 – 1988	2nd Place National Collegiate Club Hockey Tournament 26 wins, 2 losses, 0 ties
1988 – 1989	Consolation Champions National Collegiate Club Hockey Tournament 20 wins, 4 losses, 0 ties
1989 – 1990	5th Place National Collegiate Club Hockey Tournament 20 wins, 6 losses, 0 ties
1990 – 1991	2nd Place National Collegiate Club Hockey Tournament 20 wins, 7 losses, 0 ties

1991 - 1992	5th Place American Collegiate Club Hockey Tournament
	22 wins, 1 loss, 3 ties
1992 - 1993	4th Place American Collegiate Hockey Association (ACHA) National Tournament
	26 wins, 4 losses, 0 ties
1993 - 1994	4th Place ACHA National Tournament
	28 wins, 6 losses, 0 ties
1994 - 1995	7th Place ACHA National Tournament
	26 wins, 5 losses, 0 ties
1995 - 1996	7th Place ACHA National Tournament
	23 wins, 8 losses, 1 tie
1996 - 1997	4th Place ACHA National Tournament
	25 wins, 5 losses, 1 tie
1997 - 1998	8th Place (tie) ACHA National Tournament
	18 wins, 10 losses, 1 tie
1998 - 1999	5th Place ACHA National Tournament
	23 wins, 3 losses, 2 ties
1999 - 2000	5th Place ACHA National Tournament
	23 wins, 3 losses, 2 ties
2000 - 2001	8th Place ACHA National Tournament
	1st Place Fire 'n Ice Tournament, Reykjavik, Iceland
	30 wins, 4 losses, 1 tie
2001 - 2002	4th Place ACHA National Tournament
	26 wins, 4 losses, 0 ties
2002 - 2003	6th Place ACHA National Tournament
	24 wins, 6 losses, 0 ties
2003 – 2004	11 wins, 14 losses, 2 ties
2004 – 2005	13 wins, 12 losses, 1 tie
2005 – 2006	10th Place ACHA National Tournament
	21 wins, 13 losses, 0 ties
2006 – 2007	24th Place ACHA Final Season Rankings
	17 wins, 14 losses, 0 ties
2007 – 2008	22nd Place ACHA Final Season Rankings
	22 wins, 8 losses, 1 tie
2008 – 2009	14 wins, 13 losses, 2 ties
2009 – 2010	12 wins, 18 losses, 0 ties
2010 – 2011	25th Place ACHA Final Season Rankings
	14 wins, 12 losses, 3 ties

32 Year Totals			
Wins	Losses	Ties	Pct.
634	216	26	72.2%

Coming- The Icecat Chronicles

The coach, his coaches, his players, the parents, the media and The University